Lean Project Leade|

Lawrence P. Leach, President

Shane P. Leach

Advanced Projects, Inc.

6 N Ridge Drive

Boise, ID 83716

ISBN-10: 1-4392-6188-1

ISBN-13: 978-1-4392-6188-0

Contents

Preface

This book is for you if you wish to implement Lean Project Management/ Critical Chain Project Management (LPM/CCPM). While my previous books provide enough necessary knowledge to succeed with LPM/CCPM, I felt they could be improved with more graphic detail than makes sense in a primarily text media. While the training I do contains nearly all of the information presented in this book, the detailed knowledge from such training, if not implemented immediately and reinforced, often fades rapidly. Few people go back to review the slides or electronic files, and even if they do, most cannot recall much of what was said. This book's presentation format seeks to appeal to alternative learning preferences and how our visual system and brains work.

The presentation provides a series of two-page modules, as listed in the contents. The idea is to open each two page module before you, so you see the graphics on the left and the text on the right. Using both graphics and text works better with two different learning preferences. The graphics on the left are to appeal to the right brain, because your visual system processes your left field of vision with the right side of your brain, and vice versa with the text, which tends to appeal mostly to the left brain. I don't know if this idea really works, but felt one way to find out was to get it out to a large number of people, and see what they say about it. Please let me know if it works for you, or not.

Sticking to two-page modules creates a space constraint. I did not let it get too overwhelming by using from one to three figures in a module, adjusting the white space, and in a few cases, the font size, to get in what was necessary. I hope that doesn't offend the detail-minded too much.

Use the table of contents to pick out the modules that interest you, in the order that fits your needs or thinking pattern. You may wish to flip through; browsing the graphics to see what catches your interest. Here are some recommendations for different needs.

Reader	Recommended Modules
Everyone	2.x Three Rules
Most Everyone	1.x Introduction 4.x Execution
Project Manager	4.x Execution 4.x Execution 4.x Execution (Note: This is not an error!)
Scheduler	8.x Networks
LPM/CCPM Implementation Team Member	7.x Leading Change 6.x Roles
Senior Manager	7.x Leading Change 9.x Improvement 10. Future
System Thinker, Project Delivery System Owner (e.g. PMO Director)	3.x CCPM & LPM 5.x LPM

Some might desire a comment on the names LPM and CCPM. Why not pick one and stick with it? I chose the name Lean Project Management for my last book for two reasons: to force myself to incorporate more of the Lean ideas into my thinking, and to make it appeal to a wider audience. I did not want to abandon the name CCPM. It has some legs. On the other hand, the acronym has not been adopted as I had hoped. Many users apply the acronym CCPM only to critical chain in the context of the Theory of Constraints (TOC), without the strong use of the PM part from the PMBOK™; i.e. not just the guide, but all the project management literature that comprises it. I see a big problem with that, as I fear that some TOC practitioners are not well enough versed in professional project management. There are notable exceptions.

I continue to learn about Lean manufacturing and the elements of the Toyota Production System that preceded it. I have studied them extensively, and applied the principles as best I can. I have learned enough to be sure that the Lean principles fit well with the direction of CCPM and all business improvement initiatives. I feel a need to sponsor synthesizing all of the alternative approaches to business improvement, instead of defending one method as better than another. I value the areas where alternative business improvement methods seem to agree, because that supports their joint validity. I value more the areas that one set of ideas covers and another does not cover, because that expands our overall knowledge of the system. I most especially value the areas in which the improvement methods seem to conflict, because that is where I suspect the opportunities for breakthroughs lie. Since all have the same objective, the apparent disconnects tell us that our picture of the one reality that must exist is not yet complete.

Third and finally, trends in business have seemed to favor Six Sigma and Lean approaches over the Theory of Constraints (TOC). Critical chain was developed by Eli Goldratt, who developed TOC. I am not sure why TOC has not fared as well in the market for business improvement approaches, but have a few theories. One is that TOC emphasizes the necessity of real senior management leadership, while some advocates of other approaches would have you believe that you can make great improvements by assigning your Lean or Six Sigma initiatives to staff "black belts"; as if senior management doesn't have to change what they do. That seems to appeal to many senior managers. The real leaders who succeeded with those methods (e.g. Ohno, Welch) know that isn't true, but I fear that the practice in many organizations does not follow their model.

As you will see from the last module, I consider business improvement a never-ending process. Please share with me your results with this material, and your own ideas on how to further enhance the use of this material or improve the process of delivering project success while making happy stakeholders. You can reach me by email at: Larry@Advanced-projects.com.

1. Introduction

You should adopt Lean Project Management practices for only one reason: they work for you. Many have found the principles and practices described herein produced unprecedented project results in terms of overall success, no matter how measured. You can too.

Don't take anything in the pages that follow as gospel. Take it as my input to your thinking. Critically examine every assertion relative to your knowledge and experience. Relate each element to the specifics of your organization. Use what will work for you. Put the other aside, perhaps for later reconsideration. You don't have to do everything on these pages to succeed. You can come up with better solutions for your specific needs. You may find new breakthroughs that go far beyond what is presented here. When you do, please share them with me and others.

The pages that follow present a lot of detail. No one does all of it. You don't have to do all of it to get great success with LPM. You do have to cause the organization you work in to do things differently, if you hope to achieve different results. Even if those changes only affect what you do, you can have personal success. The more people you can influence, the larger the successes you will create. The large the successes you create, the more people you will be able to influence. It is like compound interest.

I first learned about project management while working as an engineer on a large government funded R&D project improving the safety of commercial nuclear power plants. For my first three years on the project, the schedule posted in the front office was renewed each year with a new picture that moved the completion date of the project out a year. At the end of the third year, the occupant of that office was given other opportunities, and the new manager took on the job of making us a project organization. He brought in the people who were best in the world at it at that time; those building nuclear submarines in Groton, Connecticut. They helped us make a real schedule, and more importantly taught us how to use it.

The project never missed another schedule. We extended the methods we learned to the rest of the work in the company, and soon became known as the best project management company in the business. , The methods we learned are very much like those in today's Project Management Body of Knowledge (PMBOK), with one important difference: they taught us to use a buffer. When I later learned of Goldratt's buffers with critical chain, it helped me understand why those methods were as successful as they were. However, I now know how to bring additional Lean and Six Sigma methods to bear in ways that would have greatly improved the success we obtained back then. And now I know why it improves success. I hope to share that knowing with you.

I have tried to structure the material to be accessible to all of you. Please let me know how it is working out. Also, please give me your improvement ideas.

Most importantly, get out there and do something.

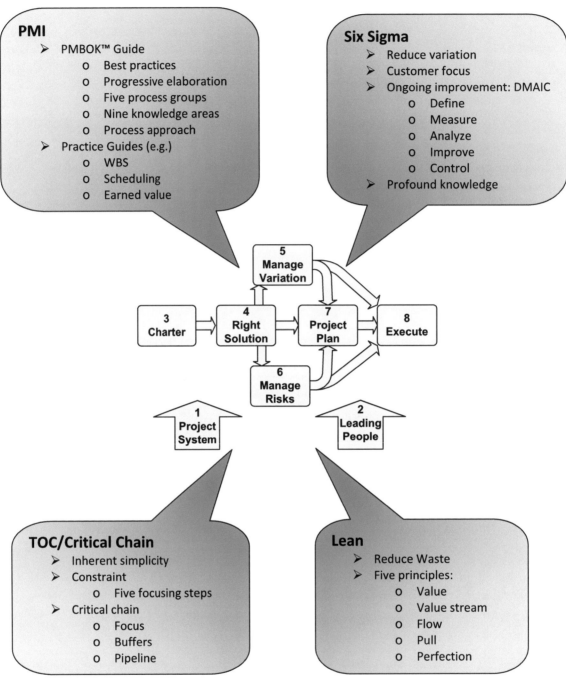

PMI
- ➤ PMBOK™ Guide
  - o Best practices
  - o Progressive elaboration
  - o Five process groups
  - o Nine knowledge areas
  - o Process approach
- ➤ Practice Guides (e.g.)
  - o WBS
  - o Scheduling
  - o Earned value

Six Sigma
- ➤ Reduce variation
- ➤ Customer focus
- ➤ Ongoing improvement: DMAIC
  - o Define
  - o Measure
  - o Analyze
  - o Improve
  - o Control
- ➤ Profound knowledge

5 Manage Variation

3 Charter

4 Right Solution

7 Project Plan

8 Execute

6 Manage Risks

1 Project System

2 Leading People

TOC/Critical Chain
- ➤ Inherent simplicity
- ➤ Constraint
  - o Five focusing steps
- ➤ Critical chain
  - o Focus
  - o Buffers
  - o Pipeline

Lean
- ➤ Reduce Waste
- ➤ Five principles:
  - o Value
  - o Value stream
  - o Flow
  - o Pull
  - o Perfection

Lean Project Management Harmonizes Perspectives to Deliver Successful Projects "In half the time, all the time".

1.1 What is Lean Project Management?

Overall Lean Project Management (LPM) seeks better ways to execute projects of all types. Module 1.2 summarizes the huge success obtained by simplifying and harmonizing the best available tools for project success: the Project Management Institute's Guide to the Project Management Body of Knowledge (PMBOK™ Guide), the Theory of Constraints (TOC) application of Critical Chain, Six Sigma process improvement, and elements of Lean production management.

The eight high-level process steps of Lean Project Management (center of the graphic) synthesize all of these elements.

Leach, L. (2005). Lean Project Management. Booksurge.

PMI The Project Management Institute (PMI) developed the PMBOK™ Guide as an international standard to improve the ***successful delivery of projects***. The PMBOK™ Guide takes a process approach to link the full body of project delivery knowledge through five process groups and nine knowledge areas. PMI continues improving its tools for project success. They:
1. Continue to improve the PMBOK™ Guide, currently working on the fourth edition,
2. Develop supplemental specialized guides (e.g. for government projects),
3. Offer a suite of practice guides (for practices such as the Work Breakdown Structure (WBS), scheduling, and Earned Value), and
4. Offer training, publications, and international collaboration.

TOC
Critical Chain TOC focuses on increasing **Throughput** of the system. TOC initially improved production processes with the Drum-Buffer-Rope (DBR) approach to increase the flow through the system constraint. Dr. Goldratt's Critical Chain scheduling and control method applies the same ideas of understanding variation, dependent events, and the constraint to improve project workflow.

Goldratt, E. (1997). Critical Chain. Great Barrington, MA: North River Press
Leach, L. (2000, 2005). Critical Chain Project Management. Boston: Artech House

Six Sigma Six Sigma deploys process improvement tools to **reduce variation.** Building on the quality movement initiated in the 1950s by Drs. W. Edwards Deming and Joseph Juran, General Electric's CEO Jack Welch made Six Sigma famous through effectively applying it to build General Electric into the greatest wealth producing engine of the world.

Lean Lean builds on the Toyota Production System (TPS), focusing on ***eliminating waste***. TPS focuses on flexibility. Lean builds on five principles to eliminate seven types of waste. It seeks to minimize Work in Progress (WIP) through applying Just In Time (JIT) supply and manufacturing.

Harmony PMI's tools, TOC, Six Sigma, and Lean sometimes overlap, assuring a strong tool or approach. They each cover some different ideas that do not conflict, combining to form a more holistic approach. The methods may seem to conflict on some things. Apparent conflicts provide opportunities to explore the assumptions of the alternative perspectives and select the approach that best meets the needs of your system.

- ➢ **Increased:**
  - o **Project success: near 100%**
  - o **Project throughput: 30-100%**
  - o **Project profits: much more than 100%**
- ➢ **Reduced:**
  - o **Project cycle time: 50% or more**
  - o **Project Work in Progress (WIP): more than 30%**
  - o **Quality defects: 50% or more**
  - o **Project cost: 10% or more**
  - o **Stress for all project stakeholders**

CCPM/LPM Improves Project Key Success Factors

Item	From:	To:
Project size	Small	Large
Project type	Knowledge work (e.g. Engineering, IT)	Heavy Construction
Organizations	Business	All types
Project length	Short (days)	Long (years)
Life cycle	R&D	Operations, Maintenance and Decommissioning
Number of projects	Single	Hundreds
Project Management Process Maturity	Low or nonexistent	Established Project Management Office (PMO) or Project Driven Process (e.g. !SO 9001)
Project Manager Skills	Ad-hoc	Project Management Professional
Work Environment	Chaos	Ordered project flow
Culture adaptability	Local	International

CCPM/LPM Success Spans a Wide Range of Organization and Project Types

1.2 Why LPM?

Summary   LPM causes huge success at delivering projects "*in half the time, all the time*". The figure illustrates the impressive improvements often achieved with LPM. Improvements include all three measures of the project "triple constraint": schedule, cost, and scope. LPM substantially improves quality and reduces stress for project stakeholders. The same relative improvement levels are often achieved regardless of project type, size, and number of projects. The initial relative improvement does not seem to depend on the initial project system maturity of the organization, but organizations with more mature project delivery systems deliver higher absolute performance.

Triple Constraint   Before LPM, many organizations and project types demonstrate success to the triple constraint on the order of 10-30%. That is, most projects either over-run schedule, over-run budget, or under-deliver scope, or a combination. (Some organizations with mature project change control systems report higher success rates to the "final" baseline triple-constraint estimates, but actually experience the same or worse level of performance relative to the initial baseline.) With LPM the success rate usually approaches 100%. More importantly, that success rate includes projects completing in half the time, at up to twice the previous completion rate, with the same resources. The number of projects in work at any time (WIP) decreases, causing further reinforcing feedback. Ultimately, improvement comes from eliminating waste: the waste of multitasking and waste of delays.

Quality   Organizations that measure quality defects during project execution show a dramatic reduction in quality defects with LPM; often on the order of 50%. Reduced quality defects cause reduced waste and rework, and thus reduce project duration and cost. The reduction in quality defects comes from reducing the task switching caused by multitasking, reducing stress, reducing cycle time, and from the closer coupling of the cause and effect of defects.

Cost   Some project organizations realize significant project cost reductions with LPM. Reducing waste, particularly task switching and quality defects, causes the reported cost reductions. From a TOC perspective, most claimed cost reductions on projects that use internal resources paid for as operating expenses are an illusion, but increases to throughput and bottom-line profit are always real. For internal resources where paid overtime is a factor, reductions in paid overtime can cause a significant real cost reduction, increasing profit.

Stress   Project stakeholders report substantially reduced stress after implementing LPM. Performing resources, task managers (supervisors), and project managers report the greatest stress reductions. Studies show that in the stress range of most organizations, stress reduction substantially increases productivity. More importantly, stress reduction greatly improves the health and well-being of project stakeholders. More has to be done to quantify these effects and further increase harmony.

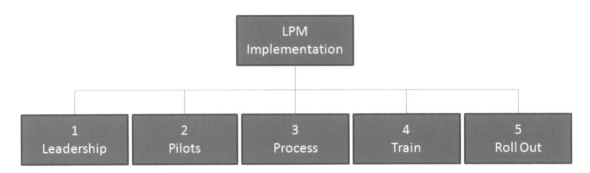

Example Work Breakdown Structure (WBS) for Implementing LPM

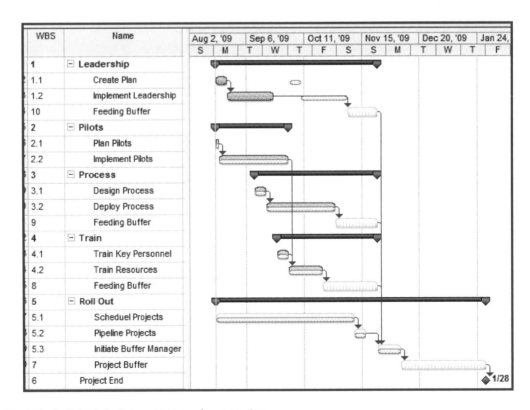

Critical Chain Schedule Drives LPM Implementation

Summary

Implement LPM as a project. As with any project, scale the implementation project plan to the size of your organization. With small organizations and direct senior leadership saying "we *are* going to do this", a project charter and critical chain schedule may suffice. The organization may be fully operational with the new behaviors in a few months. Larger organizations frequently have larger communication and culture change challenges, requiring a formal Project Plan; i.e.

> ➢ Scope statement
> ➢ Budget
> ➢ Critical Chain Schedule
> ➢ Risk Management Plan
> ➢ Communication Plan
> ➢ Change Management Process
> ➢ Issue and Action Management Process

The leadership team should appoint a project manager for the implementation. The project manager reports to the leadership team, who are the project sponsors.

Behavior

Implementing CCPM/LPM requires changing some key behaviors, starting with management. Current policies and practices, formal and informal, reinforce current behaviors. Implementation success depends critically on changing the behavior reinforcers. While training and software help a little, only behavior change causes results. Behavior change requires eliminating the reinforcers of the old behaviors and instituting reinforcers of the new behaviors, starting with the three rules, the topic of the next module.

Daniels, A. and Daniels, J. (2006). *Performance Management: Changing Behavior that Drives Organizational Effectiveness*. Atlanta, GA: Performance Management Publications.

WBS

Once chartered, the implementation team should focus first to create a Work Breakdown Structure (WBS) for the implementation. The WBS assigns responsibility to plan and execute the change. The top figure on the facing page illustrates an example typical of the content needed by most organizations. The amount of detail and effort required to bring about the deliverables will vary.

Critical Chain

The implementation team plans and executes the implementation as an LPM project. In addition to guiding the implementation, this helps the team learn the process they are implementing. Since some efforts such as coaching extend over a period of time, the critical chain schedule for implementation may not be typical of those developed for the company products. Implementation team members should show as task managers (MS Project users can adopt the Contact field for this purpose), and may also be performing resources. It might also be appropriate to use a larger project buffer than normal; i.e. on the order of 100% of the critical chain duration (vs. 50%). The figure illustrates a high-level example schedule only; your plan will differ and have many more tasks. The example shows mostly just the summary tasks, corresponding to the deliverables in the WBS.

Flowchart to define benefits from LPM/CCPM.

| | Baseline | % Change | | | Projected |
		Min	Mean	Max	Mean
Throughput	$5,000,000				
Direct Throughput Improvement		30%	50%	80%	$2,500,000
Penalties or Incentives	-$100,000				$100,000
Cost of Quality	25%	-30%	-50%	-80%	-$625,000
Effective Throughput	$3,650,000				$6,975,000
Operating Expense	$3,500,000	0%	-10%	-25%	$3,150,000
Net **P**rofit	$150,000				$3,825,000
Investment in Change	$250,000				
Return **O**n **I**nvestment	N/A				1530.00%

Investment Analysis for LPM/CCPM implementation demonstrates huge Return on Investment (ROI).
Note that the only valid reductions in operating expense come from actual cost outlay reduction; e.g. reduction in overtime or use of contracted staff. Increased capacity should ALWAYS drive to increase Throughput.

1.3.1 Calculating the Benefits

Summary
Many contemplating LPM need a calculation of benefits before they are able to proceed. You can treat the implementation of LPM as a Master Black Belt project.

TOC Perspective
Two items separate the TOC approach to benefits from those frequently applied in determining the impact of Lean or Six Sigma (or Lean Sigma) projects. First, TOC emphasizes increasing Throughput, vs. reducing cost. Second, TOC *always* focuses on the whole system, whereas the other processes often *allow* focus on elements of the system; i.e. "local improvements", in particular for green or black belt projects. Other than for cost reductions, system improvement is NOT the sum of local improvements. System improvement comes *only* from improvement at the constraint. Cost reductions have limited impact potential; there is no limit to Throughput improvement. Claimed local cost reductions often do not occur; Throughput increases are always real, and translate directly to the bottom line.

Sources of Benefits
The primary gains from LPM are due to increased Throughput of projects (30-50+%), with the same level of resources, and reduced cycle time (30-75%). Reduced cycle time can have a long-term effect by making the organization more competitive. Reduced cycle time and consequent improved predictability can also eliminate the cost of any schedule penalties the company may be paying at present and enable the collection of incentive payments in the future. Such payments are highly desirable because they drop right to the bottom line as profit. Additional beneficial effects include reduced defects (40-80%), and consequent rework, and direct cost savings per project (10-25%). Note that cost savings per project do not usually map to the bottom line profit of the company, and never do if the projects are worked by organization employees, and there is no reduction in force or overtime to cause actual operating expense reductions.

Calculation
The figure illustrates a typical calculation. You can download this spreadsheet from www.Advanced-projects.com. Adjust it for the appropriate figures in your organization. Input the baseline numbers for Throughput, the sum of any increases in Throughput due to incentives or penalties (-), and total Operating Expense. Also estimate the amount of your operating expense that goes to correcting quality errors: the cost of quality. If your organization does not track the cost of quality, it is likely in the range of 25% of Throughput. Put in your estimate. The spreadsheet will calculate profit automatically. Ensure that the profit number makes sense. Then adjust the gains projected, being mindful of the minus signs, including the net effect on incentives or penalties. The projected mean quantities will calculate automatically. 1,500% ROI will seem outrageous to many people. They are used to dealing with ROIs of a few percent, or at most a few tens of percent. Although such numbers represent the reality of success with TOC/LPM/CCPM, you may need to tone it down for acceptance in your company. Although achieving such results requires a substantial and sustained leadership effort by senior management, can anything else create this size improvement?

2. Three rules

Focus comes first. It is the cause of the huge results achieved from all improvement methods. One must first focus on causing focus itself. The second rule, Buffer, and third rule, Pipeline, are important aids to focus.

When I first learned about critical chain, the discussion addressed the critical chain itself, and how it differed from the critical path. Initial implementers put much of their energy towards critical chain tasks, and the resources working them. The idea that one had to focus on the critical chain aligned with the first two of the five focusing steps of the Theory of Constraints. Focus on the critical chain was so strong that when the PMBOK™ Guide first picked up critical chain in the Third Edition, they identified it as a "network analysis technique". The critical chain as an element of focus still remains, but it is no longer the main point. Instead, for each resource that works on a critical chain project, it is most important to focus on the task at hand, and how to execute it. While the Project Manager must pay attention to the critical chain when creating the schedule, the Project Manager's primary focus is to ensure effective execution: that people focus on the right tasks the right way, and the Project Manager leads buffer recovery when needed. For the Master Scheduler of a portfolio of critical chain projects, it is a focus on the drum resource...the constraint of multiple projects...that matters most.

When I first learned of it, I understood that critical chain was about managing variation, particularly in the light of project uncertainty, finite resources, and dependent events. It took some time for me to realize that it was the buffers and buffer management were the unique contributions that Goldratt brought to project management: not the critical chain itself. I came to know that the idea of the critical chain sequence was recommended in a paper in 1963.

The ideas of focusing on execution, and the need for pipelining projects to do that, came about several years after Goldratt introduced the critical chain for single projects. He presented a rough idea of what to do near the end of his book Critical Chain, published in 1997. Practitioners had not yet discovered the full magnitude of the waste generated by resources multitasking across several projects, nor the impact of having too much work in progress in the system. Pipelining introduced a new way of planning and executing portfolios of projects.

As CCPM reached more and more organizations, users have more frequently run into conflicts between work classified as projects and other work performed by the same resources. The other work comes in many forms. For example, sometimes it is emergency work to support customers or the company's operating plants and sometimes it is supporting company process improvement. Regardless of the source, the non-project work then also competes for the attention of the resources doing project tasks, and will break focus if not also prioritized.

The Standard Direction of Solution

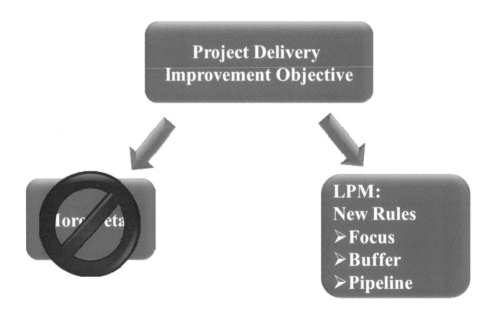

Three Rules Differentiate Lean Project Management From The Direction Most Take to Improve Project Delivery Success

Background   Systems naturally evolve towards more complexity. Several project management books now exceed 1,000 pages, and the Guide to the Project Management Body of Knowledge (not the body itself) grew to over 400 pages by its 3rd edition. Project networks have grown to tens of thousands of activities. The general idea seems to be that perhaps if we dissect and add more to what we have already sought to manage, that will make things better. People hope that more detail creates more "accurate" project plans, where accuracy represents a false belief in determinism. It never works.

Simplicity   Rather than requiring more and more detail, LPM takes an alternative direction: simplicity and focus on the flow of work to complete the project. LPM follows the critical chain direction of using the reality of variation in task duration as a management tool. This leads to three new rules for executing projects in "*half the time, all the time*": focus, buffer and pipeline. The new rules promote harmony.

Focus   Focus means performing the right tasks the right way. Initially, tasks on a project's critical chain demand focus, but once projects are going, the tasks consuming the most buffer demand focus. Performing tasks "the right way" means performing like one of the runners in a relay-race, starting as soon as the baton is handed to you, focusing 100% on the task at hand, and passing on the baton as soon as you finish your leg of the race.

Buffer   Buffers provide a discrete allowance for the variation in the execution of project tasks. Dr. Eliyahu Goldratt introduced the idea of buffer management as the primary tool to manage variation in project tasks. Although the PERT method and Monte Carlo analysis tools were used to assess variation before Goldratt, they were little used and mostly unsuccessful because they did not lead directly to management action during execution. Critical Chain buffers lead directly to two management decisions and actions:

1. Which tasks resources should work on next, and
2. When and where to take action to recover schedule buffer to complete the project by its due date.

Critical Chain's use of these decisions makes all the difference.

Pipeline   Pipelining uses the capacity of the constraint resource (aka "the drum" in TOC) to control the release of projects to the system. This minimizes the work in progress (WIP) at any time, thereby greatly improving synchronization of project work and reducing overall project duration. Pipelining delays the start of some projects so that all projects can finish sooner. Pipelining introduces the capacity constraint buffer, minimizing queues of task work for all resources by minimizing them for the most loaded resource: the constraint (or drum) resource. The capacity constraint buffer provides a tool to account for non-project work time, and non-productive time such as vacation.

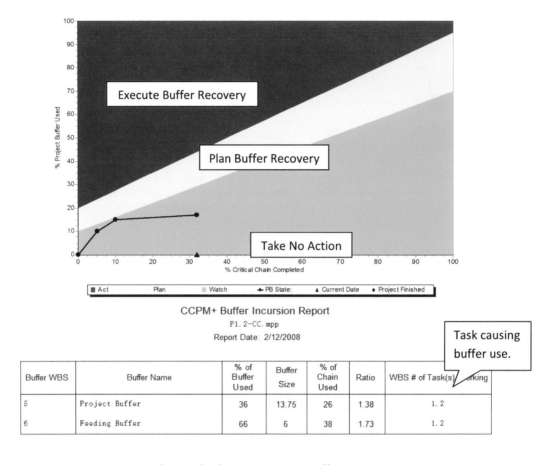

CCPM+ Buffer Incursion Report

P1. 2-CC. mpp

Report Date: 2/12/2008

Task causing buffer use.

Buffer WBS	Buffer Name	% of Buffer Used	Buffer Size	% of Chain Used	Ratio	WBS # of Task(s) Working
5	Project Buffer	36	13.75	26	1.38	1, 2
6	Feeding Buffer	66	6	38	1.73	1, 2

Buffer Management Focuses on When and Where to Recover Buffer.

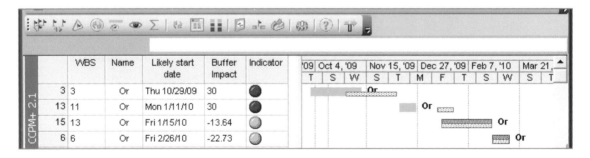

Task Managers Use Task Lists Filtered by Resource and Prioritized by Task Buffer Penetration to Dispatch Work. *Note that only tasks for resource Or are shown, and sorted by Buffer Impact. Resources work on one task at a time.*

Overall

The first rule of Lean Project Management is to focus on the flow of the value adding work, a Lean principle. Active buffer management guides project flow. Focus demands dispatching resources to the right tasks, enabling resources to focus on the task, helping resources when task completion is delayed or threatened, and taking action to recover buffers when and where necessary.

Buffer Management

Buffer Management actively engages project stakeholders to control project flow. When buffers reach predetermined action limits the project team acts to recover buffer in order to complete the project with less than 100% buffer consumption. When needed, they escalate issues and decisions for management help. When buffer use moves into the yellow region, buffer recovery planning starts by ensuring everything has been done to unstick and expedite the current working task and then develops plans to recover the lost time with tasks that comprise the chain from the working task to the project buffer. During the first half of the project buffer recovery planning seeks to bring the buffer to zero percent used at project end. The reason is that the team may not be able to accomplish all the planned recovery and other impacts that may occur along the way.

Dispatching Resources to The Right Tasks

Task managers, usually the first level supervisors, use the prioritized task list by resource to dispatch tasks for execution. All incomplete tasks have a buffer impact, whether the task has started or not. Not started tasks inherit the buffer impact from the working or just completed task in their predecessor chain. Critical chain tasks start with zero buffer penetration, and feeding chain tasks start with negative buffer penetration equal to the size of the feeding buffer. Thus, initially, critical chain tasks get precedence over feeding chain tasks. Once the pipeline of multiple projects is working, buffer use is the sole tool to set task priority. A feeding chain task may have higher priority than a critical chain task, and a task on a low priority project may have higher priority than a task on high priority project.

The Right Way

Project flow demands that resources focus on one task at a time, completing it before going back to their task list to find out which task to work on next. Tasks do not have completion dates: each task should complete and be statused as complete as soon as possible. The duration of the task input to the schedule has no meaning during execution. It was just a tool to size the buffers and set overall project duration. About half the tasks should overrun that duration and half should underrun it.

Focus on Flow

Senior management acts like the Admirals in charge of a fleet of ships (projects), and the ship Captains are in charge of individual ships (projects) Middle and Project Managers take control of their responsibility while aiding the rest of the fleet. Leadership plots the course to the objective taking into account all potential impacts on achieving the objective and provisioning the fleet to accomplish its goal. This includes checking ahead for potential storms (project risks), and ensuring the smooth operation of each ship as part of the fleet; e.g. not running into other ships (projects).

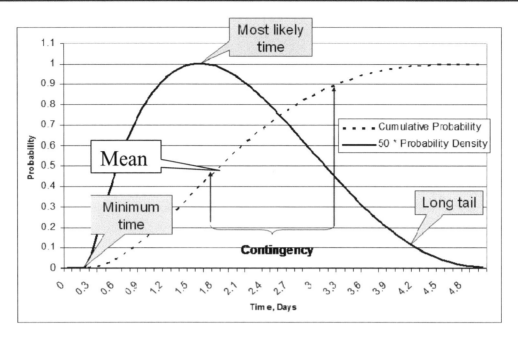

Project Task Completion Probability (x 50) and Cumulative Probability vs. Task Duration.
*Contingency is the difference between about a 50% chance (Median/most likely or mean…which are not the same) of completing the task in that duration or less, and about a 90% chance. **Accuracy** defines the range of the variation around the target (i.e. the mean).*

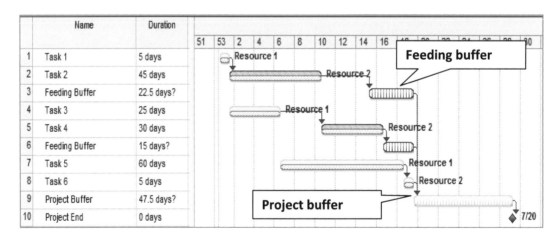

Two of the Critical Chain Buffers Appear as Tasks in Individual Project Plans. *They act like the shock absorbers in your car, damping the variation in task performance time. (The third buffer, described in section 2.4, is quite different.) Lime colored tasks comprise the critical chain.*

Buffers

Buffers are the primary innovation of critical chain. Most projects practice subtly deterministic thinking, planning each activity to complete within its estimated duration to a high probability, hoping thereby to complete the project within its planned time. This proves to be a very ineffective way to plan for and manage variation. Buffers provide the means to actively **manage** variation.

Task Variation

The actual duration of most project tasks varies. The duration of essentially similar tasks exhibit a two or three sigma variation range (95-99% of the times fall within these limits) on the order of -50% to +100% of the mean (or more!), as illustrated by the upper figure. Although there are some exceptional nearly fixed duration tasks in some projects, the large amount of variation rules for most project tasks. For this reason, predictions of single-point task duration have near zero chance of being right. Task start and finish dates have no meaning: they are pure fiction. Buffers take advantage of this reality to manage effectively.

Critical chain uses two key 'in-project' buffers: a single **project buffer** at the end of the critical chain, to protect the overall project due-date, and **feeding buffers,** illustrated on the lower figure, wherever non-critical (feeding chain) tasks feed into critical chain tasks. The feeding buffers aid task synchronization, and further protect the project due date.

Buffer Size

The project and feeding buffers come out of the tasks in the chains that feed them. Due to the mathematics of variation, it takes much less buffer to protect a chain of tasks to some probability (say 90% chance of not being exceeded) than the sum of what it takes to protect each task in the chain. You can approximate the mathematics by taking the square root of the sum of the squares of the amounts removed from each task in the chain. For long chains, the buffer amount is MUCH less than the amount removed from the tasks. Thus, adding buffers this way reduces the overall length of activity chains. Here's how I describe the method Dr. Eliyahu Goldratt suggested:

1. Estimate the mean duration of tasks as one-half of the previous (low risk) estimate,
2. Move the amounts taken from the task to a buffer at the end of the chain, and then
3. Cut that buffer in half.

This method yields project plans ~25% shorter than the resource-leveled critical path plan, with 1/3 of the total duration being the buffer.

Buffer Management

Active buffer management provides the key to critical chain success. It provides the focusing keys discussed in rule 1. In addition, using the buffers to measure and control the project flow ensures that projects complete by their due dates most of the time, and often in less than one-half of the previous time. The first graphic under rule 1 illustrated the fever chart and the associated table that guides buffer recovery actions. When buffer use is in the green region, no buffer recovery action is needed. When buffer use moves into the yellow region, the project team must plan for buffer recovery. When buffer use moves into the red region, the project team implements buffer recovery.

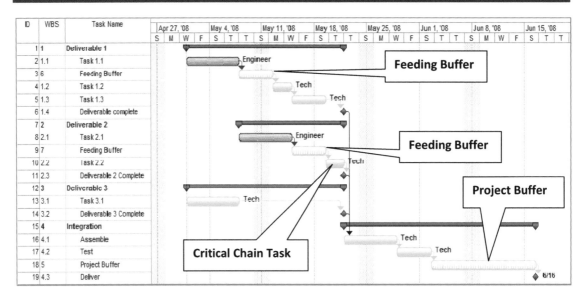

Project and Feeding Buffers Appear as Tasks in Individual Project Plans. *The project buffer sets the project delivery date. Feeding buffers aid task synchronization.*

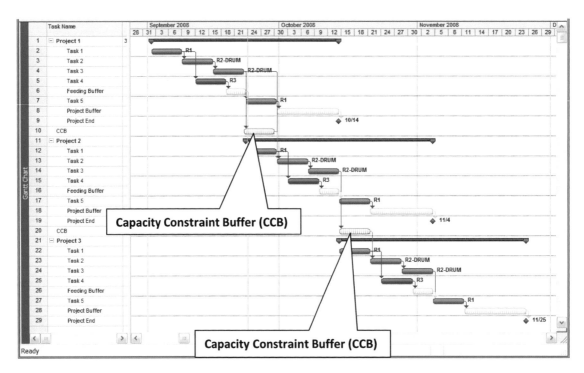

Capacity Constraint Buffer (CCB) Sets the Start Date for Projects. *The capacity constraint buffer reduces task queuing waste and accounts for non-productive time. R2 is drum resource.*

Three Schedule Buffers

Three schedule buffers:
- ➤ Provide the means to reduce waste from queuing and task desynchronization,
- ➤ Enable forward looking project control, and
- ➤ Support planning and execution decisions.

Project Buffer

The **project buffer** sets the end date for the project. Each project has one project buffer. It accounts for common-cause variation in the tasks along the critical chain, and for some external influences. The project buffer enables key project decisions.

Initially size the project buffer as 50% of the sum of the duration of the tasks along the critical chain. Do not include gaps that may exist in the critical chain. Later, you may use alternative methods:

Leach, L. (2003). *Schedule and Cost Buffer Sizing: How to Account for the Bias Between Project Performance and Your Model*. PM Journal, Vol. 24 No. 2

Feeding Buffers

Feeding buffers prevent delaying tasks on the critical chain due to waiting for inputs from non-critical chain tasks. Projects can have many feeding buffers. Feeding buffers connect a task not on the critical chain to a critical chain task successor.

The feeding buffers provide a degree of isolation from variation along the feeding chains, but cannot account for all sources of variation external to the common-cause variation of critical chain tasks. See the reference above for some of these causes.

Individuals familiar with critical path scheduling frequently confuse feeding buffers with float (or slack) in critical path plans. They are entirely different. Float derives from the difference in path lengths from single point (i.e. deterministic) task duration estimates in a critical path network. Feeding buffers account for the variation in task duration along the feeding chains. Feeding buffer size varies directly with the length of the non-critical chain, whereas float varies inversely with the length of the non-critical chain. Feeding buffer location usually differs from the location of free float in a critical path plan.

Size the feeding buffers as you size the project buffer, but using the tasks in the longest branch of the feeding chain.

Capacity Constraint Buffer

The ***capacity constraint buffer*** ensures that the *constraint* to the throughput of a portfolio of projects (called the drum resource) can process all work with minimal queue build-up. The capacity constraint buffer does not appear in project schedules: it aids in setting the project start date. See 2.4 for detail on the pipelining process and a different approach for deploying the capacity constraint buffer when there are multiple units of the drum resource.

Since the capacity constraint buffer provides protective capacity for the most loaded resource across all of the projects, it ensures more protective capacity for all of the non-constraint resources. Therefore, the pipelining process can allow temporary overloads of the non-constraint resources across the portfolio.

The capacity constraint buffer should be on the order of 50% of the availability of the constraint (see 2.4).

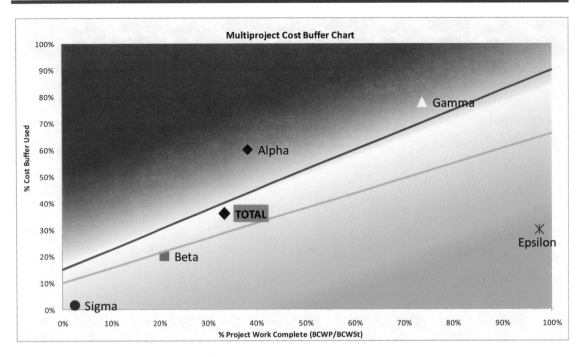

Cost Buffer Multiproject Fever Chart Enables Cost Management. *The cost buffer abscissa uses Earned Value (EV) to measure "% complete" as the summed EV for completed tasks divided by the total mean task cost estimated (the task budget). EV sums the* **budgeted cost** *for the work completed.*

#	Project	% Cpl	Buffer	BASELINE			CURRENT			EAC	
				BCWSt	CB	BAC	BCWS	BCWP	ACWP	Min*	Max*
1	Alpha	38%	60%	$39,288	$10,000	$49,288	$21,000	$15,000	$21,000	$45,288	$55,003
2	Beta	21%	20%	$10,000	$2,500	$12,500	$2,000	$2,100	$2,600	$10,500	$12,381
3	Gamma	74%	78%	$39,340	$9,000	$48,340	$30,000	$29,000	$36,000	$46,340	$48,836
4	Delta	47%	-23%	$55,000	$13,000	$68,000	$25,000	$26,000	$23,000	$52,000	$48,654
5	Epsilon	98%	30%	$20,000	$5,000	$25,000	$19,000	$19,500	$21,000	$21,500	$21,538
6	Sigma	3%	2%	$120,000	$30,000	$150,000	$2,000	$3,000	$3,500	$120,500	$140,000
7											
8											
9											
	TOTAL	33%	36%	$283,628	$34,750	$318,378	$99,000	$94,600	$107,100	$296,128	$321,105
	CB Factor	0.5									

Cost Buffer Table Predicts Estimate at Complete. *The right column prints in red if the proportional prediction exceeds the BAC: sum of the task budget plus individual project cost buffer.*

Cost Buffer

LPM recommends focusing on the schedule for control. Some situations (e.g. projects performed on a contract basis) require separate cost management. The cost buffer ensures that projects complete within their budgeted amount, while minimizing the cost estimate and actual cost for the entire project. The same statistical laws that apply to schedule buffers apply to project cost. Applying a single cost buffer for the project, vs. estimating each task cost to not exceed its estimate, has the same effect as applying a single schedule buffer, reducing the total of individual estimates plus buffer.

Individual Project Cost Buffers

Individual project cost buffers are similar to individual project schedule buffers. The project task costs are estimated as mean values, and the buffer protects the sum of the cost from all tasks in the project. The total budget for the project, Budget at Completion (BAC) sums the total for the task estimates and adds the cost buffer. Because there are more tasks summed than in a schedule buffer; i.e. all the tasks in the project vs. only the tasks along a chain, the cost buffer can usually be smaller, as a percent of the baseline, than a schedule buffer. See the reference for sizing suggestions.

Track the single project cost buffers with single project cost buffer charts. The abscissa for the cost buffer chart is the % of the project that is complete, estimated using the Earned Value (EV) for completed tasks as a percent of the total task budget for the project.

The ordinate on the cost buffer is the Cost Variance (CV) as a percentage of the total cost buffer established for the project. The Cost Variance equals the Earned Value minus the actual cost (AC).

Note: Older Earned Value terminology used the following:
- EV = Budgeted Cost of Work Performed (BCWP)
- AC = Actual Cost of Work Performed (ACWP)
- CV = ACWP-BCWP

Leach, L. (2003). *Schedule and Cost Buffer Sizing: How to Account for the Bias Between Project Performance and Your Model*. PM Journal, Vol. 24 No. 2

Total Cost Buffer

As with schedule buffers, some amount of cost variation is systematic (bias), and some amount is random. While systematic cost impacts (e.g. inflation, local area impacts not estimated correctly) sum linearly, random variation in actual cost, including those resulting from random variation in task duration, sum as the square root of the sum of the squares. This means the cost buffer for a group of projects can be less than the sum of the cost buffers necessary for each project. The table at the left allows for a simple multiplier of the sum of the individual cost buffers to create a **total cost buffer**. This is the amount necessary for the entire project portfolio. If the portfolio contains a number of projects, and if the consequences of total cost overrun are not catastrophic, I recommend starting with this factor at 0.5, and adjusting it based on experience.

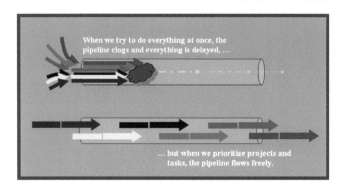

Rule 3 Pipelines All Projects. *Delaying the start of some projects accelerates the completion of all projects.*

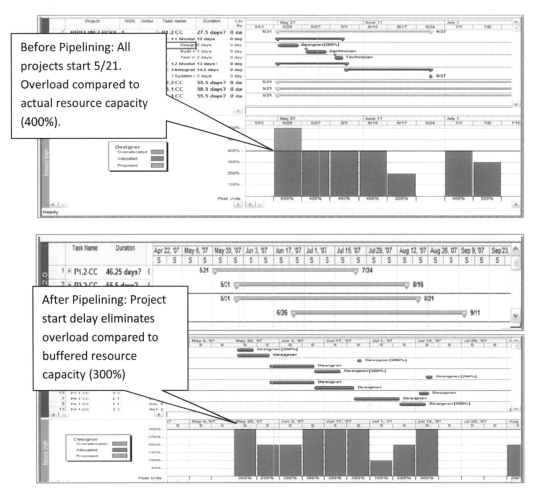

Pipelining Delays the Start of Projects to Allow for a Capacity Constraint Buffer for the Drum Resource. *The capacity constraint buffer (here set as 25%) accounts for all resource demands, including non-productive time, and provides protective capacity to minimize task delay.*

Pipeline

Pipelining plans the start of projects to accelerate completion. Planned start of projects contrasts with most organizations' approach to start projects whenever someone else dictates. Pipelining ensures that the constraint can process all the work with minimal queue (delay) build-up. Minimizing queues enables focusing on the right work, and working it the right way. Controlling the flow for the most loaded resource (the constraint) ensures the flow of work for all resources. Pipelining reduces the amount of Work in Process (WIP), and therefore decreases project duration and increases the rate of project completion.

Pipelining is not intuitive to most people. It requires delaying the start of some projects to accelerate the completion of all projects.

The Drum

The resource that is most loaded relative to its capacity over all of the projects is the *capacity constraint*, or *drum.* Project start dates derive from not overloading the drum resource, allowing for the *capacity constraint buffer*. The drum often is, but need not be, a human resource (skill). It could be a work space, a type of task (e.g. assembly and test), or a facility that has limited capacity. Management must select the drum for the purpose of scheduling the start of projects. The drum may change as project mix changes.

Project Priority

Management sets the priority for all work that accesses the drum resource. This includes all project work, and may include other work that the drum resource must perform; e.g. on-call maintenance work. Work can only enter the system through the priority process. Often externally imposed due dates provide a natural priority. If not, or if that leads to conflicts in scheduling, management must set the priority for pipelining. Maintaining project priority is an ongoing management responsibility. Frequent changes in priority cause chaos.

Capacity Constraint Buffer

The *capacity constraint buffer* ensures that the drum can process all work with minimal queue build-up. Plan individual projects assuming 100% resource availability to a common work calendar. Then use the capacity constraint buffer to account for non-productive time; e.g. vacation, sick leave, training, and other administrative time. The capacity constraint buffer also provides protective capacity so that queues do not become too large when the work presents short-term overloads to the drum resource.

The capacity constraint buffer does not appear in a project plan, but is used at the organizational level to set the start date for projects.

Maintain the Pipeline

Pipelining is an ongoing process. Management assigns one person, often called the "Master Scheduler", to maintain the pipeline. Projects complete and are removed from the pipeline, and new projects can only enter the system through the pipeline. The Master Scheduler performs "What if?" analysis, to determine a preferred solution to match the organization performance capability to the work demands.

3. CCPM & LPM

CCPM and LPM are about synthesis. I believe I coined the acronym CCPM in a presentation at a Project Management Institute forum in Long Beach CA in 1998. Critical chain was a new thing on the block, and the seminar room was filled to standing room only with over 250 people. They were experienced project managers, and their perspective was what I intended: critical chain (CC) was a logical improvement to the existing project management (PM) body of knowledge. I also had in mind that its reliance on an understanding of variation fit with the ideas of Total Quality Management (TQM), which I had been applying for about ten years at that time.

Since that time, the acronym has taken hold. Alas, I find many do not use it as I intended, but instead think of it as just the Theory of Constraints (TOC) elements of critical chain. Some have tried to position critical chain as a replacement for conventional project management. I have found that they do not understand the science of project management. Fortunately, others have realized that the TOC approach was incomplete by itself, and began to add back in some of the necessary elements of PM; albeit with names that sound strange to professional Project Managers, such as "full kitting".

The continued development of TQM into Six Sigma, and the maturation of Lean manufacturing ideas have continued to draw my interest over the intervening years. I described my approach to apparent conflicts between differing ways to improve in the introduction. It is clear to me that Six Sigma has much yet to add to successful project delivery and the elimination of waste and introduction of system flexibility that the Lean ideas attack can also have a huge positive impact. The more I learned of Lean, the more excited I became over what it can add to PM. I have started that journey with the idea of Lean Project Management, and ask you to help me on the way.

I don't think that the journey of improving project management has an end, and I certainly do not think that the material presented in this book is the end of a road in general, much less for all specific organizations and projects. I offer these ideas as a stopping place along the way; a place for you to help me to create a better future for all.

I have also come to realize that one cannot treat only projects in an organization where the resources do both project and non-project work. Switching a mixed organization's method of project delivery, without affecting the priority and methods of accomplishing the other work, has little impact. The core problem of such organizations is a lack of a priority system for all work. The solution must resolve priorities for all work to enable effective work on both project and non-project tasks.

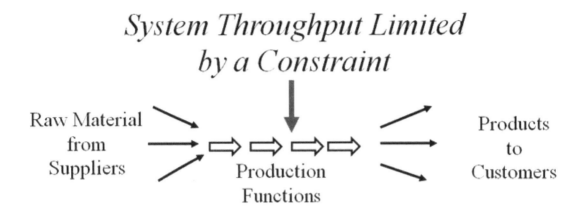

System Throughput Limited by a Constraint

Raw Material from Suppliers → Production Functions → Products to Customers

Goal: *Make money, now and in the future.*

The Theory of Constraints States That a Constraint Controls System Throughput

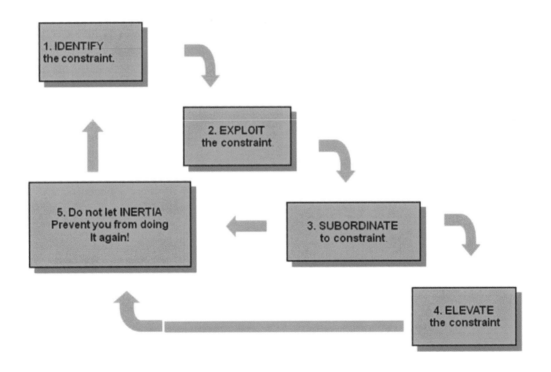

1. IDENTIFY the constraint.

2. EXPLOIT the constraint.

3. SUBORDINATE to constraint.

4. ELEVATE the constraint

5. Do not let INERTIA Prevent you from doing It again!

Goldratt's Five Focusing Steps Apply TOC Day-to-day for Ongoing Improvement

3.1 Theory of Constraints

The Goal

Dr. Eliyahu Goldratt introduced the Theory of Constraints (TOC) in *The Goal*. Written as a novel, *The Goal* takes readers through a journey of discovering how to improve a complex system by realizing an underlying inherent simplicity. The goal of a for-profit company is to make money, now and in the future. The system constraint controls progress towards that goal. Only improvements in the throughput of the constraint support the goal. This understanding leads naturally to five steps to create a process of ongoing system improvement.

Goldratt, E. (1984). *The Goal*. Great Barrington, MA: North River Press

Measures

For-profit companies measure goal achievement by the rate of profit generation. Profit fuels growth. Goldratt defined three measures to enable local decisions that support the goal:

Throughput (**T**): The rate at which the system generates money through sales. T equals revenue minus raw material cost.

Inventory (**I**): All the money the system invests in purchasing things the system intends to sell. Inventory includes both capital assets and conventional Work In Progress (WIP).

Operating Expense (**OE**): All the money the system spends in turning inventory into throughput.

Net Profit (NP) = T − OE, and Return on Investment (ROI) = NP/I. Analysis of these measures demonstrates quickly that focusing on increasing T is much more important than reducing OE or I, and that reducing I is more important than reducing OE.

Goldratt, E. (1990). *The Haystack Syndrome*. New York: North River Press

Five Focusing Steps

Goldratt introduced the Five Focusing Steps as the day-to-day process to implement TOC. Only improvements to the throughput of the constraint affect the system bottom line, therefore one must first identify the constraint. The next two steps provide the major innovation of TOC: one should first look for ways to exploit the constraint, i.e. make it more productive. TOC demonstrates that nearly all systems have huge amounts of unused capacity. Managers just don't know how to find and use it. Exploiting the constraint usually requires subordinating local measures that interfere with exploitation such as keeping workers or machines busy all the time. Only after exploiting and subordinating as far as possible should one elevate the constraint, which means offloading work from it, or getting more of it.

Ongoing Improvement

A system always has a constraint. Thus, improving throughput of the current constraint means eventually another constraint will control. One then applies the process over again. TOC provides a logical path to focus ongoing system improvement.

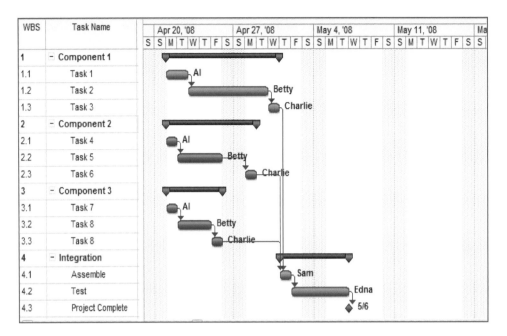

The Critical Path Method (CPM) Uses the Longest Path Through the Project Network, Without Considering the Resource Constraint. *It allows planned resource overload.*

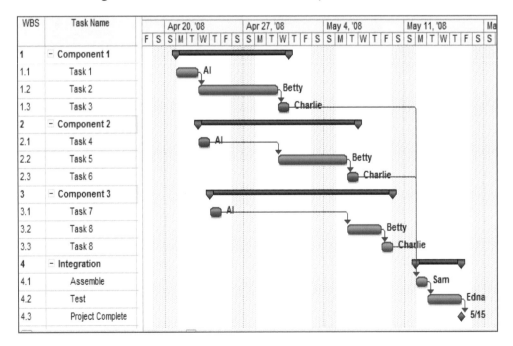

The Critical Chain of a Project: Longest Path Through the Project, After Resource Leveling. *Resource leveling ensures that the initial schedule does not plan to overload any resource. Notice how the critical chain jumps paths on resource Betty.*

Critical Chain

The Critical Chain of a project is the longest path through the network considering both task relationships and finite resource supply. It can also be called the "resource leveled critical path". The number of tasks on the critical chain usually exceeds the number of tasks on the project critical path. The critical chain may jump from one project network path (chain) to another when the predecessor and successor tasks use the same resource. If sufficient resources are available, the critical chain can be the same path of activities as the critical path.

Research revealed that the critical chain idea was proposed by Wiest in 1963, noting, "Unlike a critical path, a critical sequence is determined not by just the technological ordering and the set of job times [task durations], but also by resource constraints" (p. 396). E. Goldratt made it popular in 1997 with his novel, *Critical Chain*.

Wiest, (1963). *Some Properties of Schedules for Projects With Limited Resources.* Silver Springs, MD.: Operations Research, Inc.

Goldratt, E. (1997). Critical Chain. Great Barrington, MA: North River Press

Resource Loading and Leveling

Identifying the critical chain of a project plan requires estimating the resource demand for each task in a project schedule. This process is called "resource loading" the schedule. You may identify resources by generic type, e.g. "Engineer" or "Physical Chemist", or by individual names. For larger organizations where multiple people possess similar skills, using resource skills provides more execution flexibility.

The availability or supply of each resource must also be established. Using individual names assumes "100 %" availability for each resource. Task resource demand (loading) may be specified at any percentage or fraction. Critical Chain demands that the resource determining the task duration should be specified in increments of 100%. Next, "resource level" the network to ensure that the demand for resources within the single project does not exceed the supply.

It can be mathematically difficult to find an optimum (i.e. shortest overall duration) resource-leveled network. Understanding variation leads one to realize critical chain only requires a reasonably good solution. Scheduling programs use algorithms for resource leveling, offering the user choices. Experience in assigning resources and applying these algorithms leads to satisfactory results.

Identifying the Critical Chain

Identifying the critical chain after resource leveling requires a "backwards pass" through the network, ensuring that there are no gaps or slack. The critical chain must follow the network relationships or "jump" the network relationship path to a predecessor task using the same resource as the successor path.

Optimization of the critical chain to reduce overall project duration is usually desirable. Tasks on the critical chain should be vital to the project result. If the critical chain is controlled by resources rather than task logic, those resources should not be easily elevated; i.e. increased or off-loaded. If possible, tasks with high variability should be kept off the critical chain, because the other project chains receive additional buffering. Multiple critical chains of the same length are possible. The software algorithms usually pick one for you, and allow manual adjustment later.

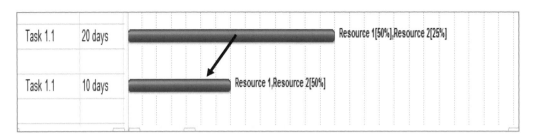

First Exploit Resources: Eliminate Planned Multitasking Affecting Task Duration. *Adjust task durations so that the resource which drives task duration is in increments of 100%; adjust others accordingly.*

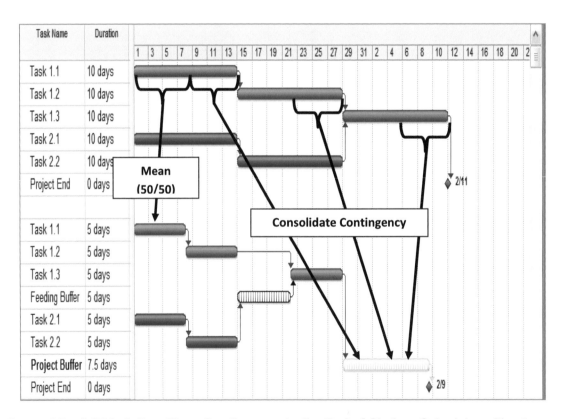

Second Exploit Variation: Move Contingency to the End of Chains. *Schedules without buffers must plan each task to high probability completion duration. CC plans use the mean task duration; i.e. about a 50% chance of completing the task within the estimated duration. See 2.3 for definition of contingency.*

Exploit

The Critical Chain of a project is the constraint to achieving the project benefits sooner. Throughput, profitability, and return on investment (ROI) increase if projects complete sooner, once started. Work in Progress (WIP) decreases in proportion to project duration; thus providing potentially huge benefits to non-profit organizations that tie up expensive equipment for maintenance and repair projects. Thus, exploiting the critical chain supports the goal of most organizations.

Five primary steps aid exploiting the critical chain at the scheduling stage of most projects:

1. Plan individual tasks to the shortest possible duration by eliminating multitasking for the resource that drives task duration,
2. Plan tasks at their 50/50 (median) duration estimates,
3. Ensure tasks on the critical chain need to be in the task sequence,
4. Reduce resource-driven sequences, and
5. Eliminate gaps in the critical chain introduced by buffer insertion.

The task scheduling changes aid exploiting task performance during execution. See 8.3.2 for discussion of items 3-5.

Note that pipelining of individual projects in a multiproject environment exploits the potential resource constraint at the multiproject system level.

Human Behavior

Exploiting the critical chain by enabling resources to focus on one task at time (aka relay-racer task behavior) measurably impacts task performance. Studies show losses (waste) of up to 40% of a person's time when engaging in task switching. Research also shows that task switching causes mistakes. Enabling single task at a time focus reduces overall quality defects on the order of 50%; possibly more for highly intellectual work. Many people exhibit certain behaviors when given dates for the delivery of results; e.g. not turning in work completed early (aka Parkinson's law: work expands to fill the available time), or not starting work in earnest on tasks until the due date seems imminent (aka Student Syndrome). CC planning seeks to eliminate these date-driven behaviors in execution by not providing completion dates for tasks; instead relying on buffer management to provide appropriate motivation to complete tasks as soon as possible.

Statistical Laws

Statistical laws support scheduling to 50/50 (median) task completion durations, with buffers, because LPM includes active task management and buffer recovery. Because project tasks tend to have a probability tail to the right, using mean estimates can lead to too long a schedule. The variation along a chain of tasks sums statistically as the square root of the sum of the squares of each individual task variation. This means it takes much less total contingency to protect a chain of tasks to the same probability of completion compared to the sum of the contingency necessary to protect each task to that same level of probability. Practically, this means over-runs on some tasks can be absorbed by under-runs on other tasks. The lower figure illustrates how this effect causes shorter project schedules, even with the addition of buffers.

A second statistical law, the *Central Limit Theorem*, ensures that the statistical distribution for the completion of a chain of tasks approaches a normal distribution, even if the individual task distributions are not normal, and differ from each other. This greatly increases the probability of completing the project within the buffered duration.

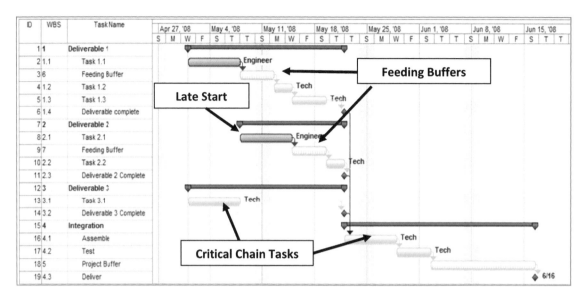

Subordinate to the Critical Chain by Inserting Feeding Buffers After Non-Critical Chain Predecessor Tasks With Critical Chain Successor Tasks. *Then, late-start the feeding chains (in the schedule) as allowed by the feeding buffers and resource-leveling. Feeding chains are allowed to start early during execution if enabled by resource availability and the prioritized task list.*

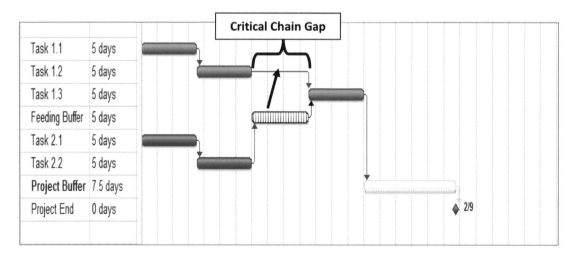

Inserting Feeding Buffers Can Cause Gaps in the Critical Chain. *Try to remove gaps during schedule optimization (see 8.3.2). Remaining gaps are a necessary part of the schedule network as planned, but can be ignored in execution.*

3.2.2 Subordinate to the Critical Chain

Subordinate

Subordination of non-critical chain work to the critical chain occurs in both the schedule and during execution. Subordination means that non-critical chain tasks are subordinate; i.e. generally should be performed after critical chain tasks whenever conflicts arise. Subordination eliminates a major cause of task start delay. Relay racer task performance rules: work on one task at a time until it is complete. The schedule must reflect this.

Schedule

Subordination of non-critical chain tasks to critical chain tasks uses feeding buffers. Feeding buffers consolidate the contingencies removed from the tasks in the feeding chain, in the same way that the project buffer consolidated the contingency removed from the critical chain tasks. The feeding buffers greatly aid task synchronization; i.e. reduce the waste of a resource waiting for an input to start a task.

Late-starting of feeding chains against the feeding buffers also aids in subordinating to the critical chain. Late-starting means moving the start of the feeding chain as far to the right as possible without affecting the project end date, and without causing resource overloads. Most critical path schedules default to early-start task positioning. This causes unnecessary pressure on resources to perform tasks earlier than they need to be performed. Late starting of tasks implements the Lean idea of pulling tasks into execution, vs. pushing them into execution.

Inserting feeding buffers can cause gaps in the critical chain. These gaps are necessary for the network as planned to ensure task synchronization. Optimization of the network should seek to minimize these gaps, but it is fine for a critical chain schedule to have such gaps. The gaps do not affect the sequence of task execution, because the execution priority derives from the actual impact of task performance on the buffers during work execution.

Size feeding buffers using the same rule as you use for the project buffer. I recommend starting out by sizing the buffers as 50% of the sum of the tasks in the chain. If feeding chains diverge upstream, use the longest path.

Execute

Subordination during execution uses prioritized task lists. Task priority derives from the statused pipelined schedules. Highest priority goes to the tasks causing the most project buffer consumption. This priority applies equally across multiple projects.

Sometimes during project execution one of the feeding chains will experience sufficient delay to cause the maximum project buffer penetration. Although feeding buffers render this infrequent, in that case resources must subordinate critical chain tasks to the appropriate feeding chain tasks. Task prioritization according to the effect on the project buffer, without regard to whether the task was initially on the critical chain or not, automatically ensures correct subordination.

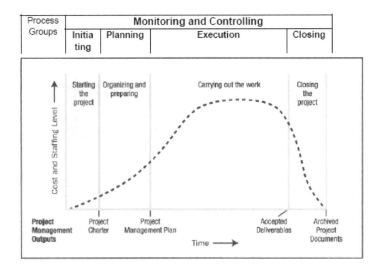

The Project Management Body of Knowledge (PMBOK™) Considers Five Process Groups. *Monitoring and controlling applies to the four overlapping project phases. (After PMI, 2008, p, 16)*

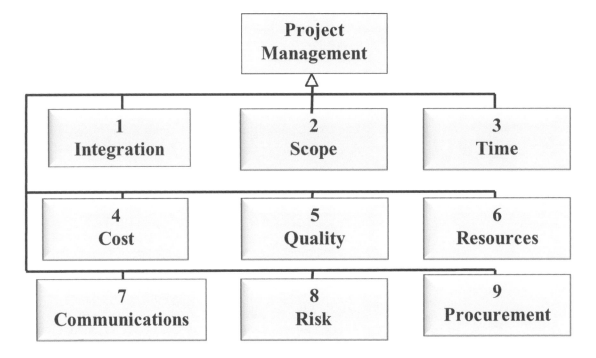

The PMBOK Guide Organizes Nine Knowledge Areas. *It develops and relates the work processes that comprise each group.*

3.3 PMBOK

PMBOK™

Lean Project Management (LPM) embraces the PM part of CCPM, which in turn deploys knowledge from professional project delivery. The PMBOK™ Guide, published by the Project Management Institute (PMI), provides the global standard for successful project planning and execution. It is an American National Standards Institute (ANSI) Standard. The fourth edition was published in 2008. Over two million copies have been distributed worldwide.

The PMBOK™ Guide seeks, as the name implies, to be a guide to vast area of knowledge. Although it seeks to identify best practices over the full range of project variables, it does not seek to prescribe what is necessary for any given project.

The general organization takes a process approach, organizing first to the phases of projects, and then to the nine knowledge areas identified as most relevant to project success.

Because it seeks to identify common practices it is not necessarily a leading guide for new practices such as CCPM or LPM. It can take quite a long time for new ideas to penetrate the industry enough to be deemed common practices. The third edition of the PMBOK Guide does acknowledge critical chain, although in much too narrow a context ("a network analysis approach")

PMI (2008). *A Guide to the Project Management Body of Knowledge. Newtown Square, PA: Project Management Institute*

Standards

PMI currently has four standards, due to be issued in "harmonized" version in December, 2008:

- ➤ *PMBOK® Guide*—Fourth Edition
- ➤ *The Standard for Program Management*—Second Edition
- ➤ *The Standard for Portfolio Management*—Second Edition
- ➤ *OPM3® (Organization Project Management Maturity Model)*—Second Edition

The PMBOK Guide uses a process description approach to describe the knowledge areas. This entails identifying the inputs, outputs, and value adding steps within each identified process. It also identifies links to other processes.

Certification

The Project Management Institute certifies professionals as possessing knowledge and skills in a variety of areas related to project leadership and execution. As of this writing, over 200,000 PMPs hold current certifications. Certification has become a minimum qualification for project managers of a certain size project in several large corporations. Current PMI credentials include:

- ➤ Certified Associate in Project Management (CAPM)
- ➤ PMI Scheduling Professional (PMI-SP)
- ➤ PMI Risk Management Professional (PMI-RMP)
- ➤ Project Management Professional (PMP)
- ➤ Program Management Professional (PgMP)

Each involves certification requirements and proficiency maintenance. While such certifications do not ensure individual performance, they set a minimum standard for knowledge and experience.

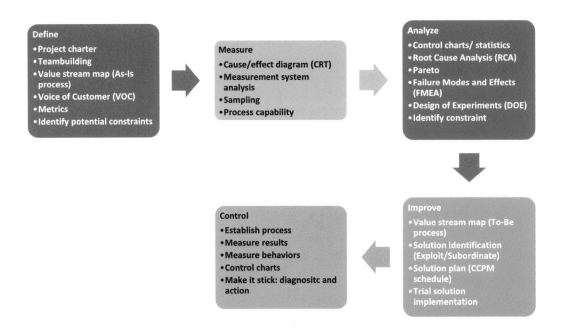

The DMAIC Process Applies to Improve the Overall Project Delivery Process (The LPM Process), and to the Individual Task Processes. *There is a similar Design for Six Sigma (DFSS) approach, DMADV.*

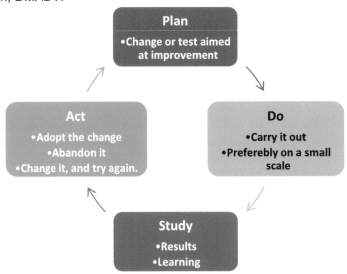

The Plan, Do, Study, Act Process Drives Continuous Improvement. *Deming called it the Shewhart cycled. Japan calls it the Deming cycle. Deming originally called it the PDCA (Check) cycle. DMAIC elaborates on it.*

Six Sigma

Six Sigma is the continuation of the quality movement which most trace back to W. Edwards Deming, Dr. Joseph Juran and others visiting Japan in 1950. Deming traces it back further to Dr. Walter Shewhart, the inventor of control charts. The idea is to manage the reality of variation to satisfy customers and build your business.

The Six Sigma idea per se traces to Motorola in the 1990s, and was made famous by Jack Welch's leadership applying it at G.E.

Leadership

Six Sigma creates huge results when led by knowledgeable, involved senior leaders who make it their agenda. Effective senior leaders define their jobs as the design and improvement of the organization processes, and leave the day-to-day operation to the employees hired for that purpose.

Many senior managers, even in very large organizations, fail to internalize this idea. They grab onto Six Sigma (and/or Lean) as an opportunity to train staff members as "belts" (green, yellow, black, master, etc.), and keep on doing what they were doing before. This approaches yields small successes, but little bottom-line impact.

It does work to deploy Six Sigma together with LPM/CCPM. There are few apparent conflicts. If there appear to be conflicts, those are opportunities to improve your system.

You do not "install" Six Sigma, any more than you "install" LPM/CCPM. You make it your way of life. Or not.

Sigmas

Sigma refers to the measure of variation of a distribution. The number of points that fall within so many sigma of the mean determines how effective a process is. Before Six Sigma, process control usually sought to control to three sigma, which allows for less than one percent defects. Six Sigma extends the "allowable" defects to one per 3.4 million opportunities, accounting for some shift in the process mean. This means the variation must be greatly reduced compared to past processes.

DMAIC

DMAIC is the primary improvement process deployed for Six Sigma. The illustration lists the steps, and some of the key features and tools that associate with each step.

Application

Six Sigma applies at the overall project delivery process level (module 5.1), and to each of the processes that comprise tasks in project plans. It applies to the design of new processes, and the improvement of existing processes. The primary thing to ensure is that you take the system approach to improvement. Process improvement must focus on the goal, and therefore on the constraint to overall value flow to the customer.

PDSA

Deming's PDSA process (illustrated) is a simpler version of the DMAIC process, and is perfectly usable. The keys to the process are:
1. It never ends. Each improvement sets the stage for the next.
2. It tests the improvement and adjusts before full-scale deployment.

Testing enables the process to work on complex systems with feedback.

Deming, W. E. (1993). The New Economics. Cambridge, MA: MIT Press, p. 94 ff.

System	Variation	Psychology	Knowledge	Lean Project Management Features
				Project Delivery System Design and Implementation
√			√	Processes
√				Policies
√				Procedures
√	√	√	√	Waste Elimination (Kaizen events)
√		√		Roles
√	√	√		Measures
	√	√		Reinforcement
			√	Ongoing Improvement (POOGI, PDSA, DMAIC, etc.)
				Project Planning
√			√	Task networks
	√	√		Mean task estimates
√		√		Task Manager assignments
	√			Project Buffer (aggregated)
	√			Feeding Buffer (synchronization)
√	√			Project Risk Management
√	√			Drum (TOC)
√	√			Capacity Constraint Buffer (Queuing)
√		√		Pipeline (WIP Control)
				Project Execution
√	√			Six Sigma
√		√		Task focus (Relay racer)
√	√	√		Prioritized task lists (focus)
√		√		Frequent task status
√	√	√		Fever chart (Visual control)
√	√	√		Project chain view (Visual control)
√	√	√		Buffer recovery
√	√	√	√	Ongoing Improvement (POOGI, PDSA, DMAIC, etc.)

LPM Features and Key SoPK Interactions. *Only the key interactions are noted. All features involve some degree of each area of Profound Knowledge.*

SoPK

W. Edwards Deming identified the System of Profound Knowledge (SoPK) as, "a map or theory by which to understand and optimize the organizations that we work in, and thus to make a contribution to the whole country (p. 94). He defined the system as four interrelated parts:

➢ Appreciation for a System
➢ Psychology
➢ Knowledge about Variation
➢ Theory of Knowledge

While one may add to this list, it certainly comprises a necessary set. Deming notes the elements cannot be separated, and that "Profound Knowledge comes from outside the system…a system cannot understand itself (p. 104).

Deming, W. E. (1993). The New Economics. Cambridge, MA: MIT Press, p. 94 ff.

System

Deming first points out that a system must have an Aim, which is the same as the Goal of TOC. He defines a system as a "network of interdependent components that work together to try to accomplish the aim of the system". We are most concerned with dynamic and non-linear business systems which are usually controlled by many feedback loops. Peter Senge's work provides an excellent route into understanding such systems.

Senge, P. (1990). The Fifth Discipline. New York: Doubleday

Psychology

Deming focused on psychology as, "a means to understand people, interactions between people and circumstances, and any system of management" (p.110). He emphasized that all business systems rely on people's behavior. A thorough science of human behavior now supports applying key principles to improve human systems. The Daniels led the field in how to apply the knowledge.

Daniels, A. and Daniels, J. (2006). Performance Management. Atlanta, GA: Performance Management Publications

Variation

Understanding variation starts with understanding that everything varies, and that there is no "true value" of anything. Classifying variation into common-cause, that which is natural to the system, and special-cause, that which can be economically removed from the system, starts the journey. Wheeler provides many key insights on how to apply understanding variation.

Wheeler, D. (2000). Understanding Variation. Knoxville, TN: SPC Press

Knowledge

A theory of knowledge ensures data-driven decisions and actions that match the real world as closely as possible. The scientific method, best described by Popper, clarifies how to develop and apply effective knowledge. Pursuit of the Philosophy of Science will inform you of some surprising things about what we know and what we don't know.

Popper, K. (1979). Objective Knowledge. Oxford, UK: Oxford University Press

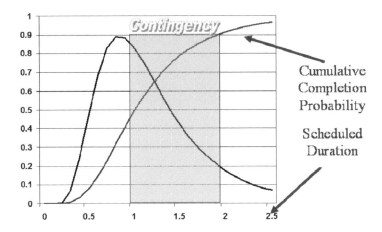

Project Tasks Experience Variation. *The abscissa is time: days or weeks. The blue curve illustrates variation on the order of -50% to +50% of the mean; typical for many project tasks.*

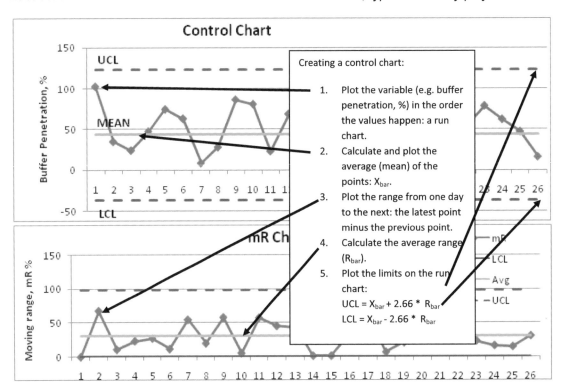

Control Charts Enable Appropriate System Decisions. *The control chart limits show common-cause variation. Management must change the process to reduce that variation. Points outside the control limits signal likely special causes, which the process operators (with management help) can work to reduce.*

3.4.2 Understanding Variation

Purpose
Understanding variation enables reality-based decisions and effective predictions. Dr. Deming noted,
"If I had to reduce my message for management to just a few words, I'd say it all had to do with reducing variation."
Designing and improving the system to achieve its goal is management's primary job. Reduce variation is a key strategy towards that goal.

Stable Process
Management of variation becomes possible when system variation is stable. Such a system is in "statistical control". You can make predictions for such a system with reasonable certainty (never 100%). Assuming you can make more "accurate" predictions by using more detail in your project plans demonstrates a lack of understanding variation and does not work! Do you know if your project delivery system is stable?

Common-cause and Special-cause
A system in statistical control usually shows only what is known as common-cause variation; i.e. random variation inherent in the system itself. Faults from fleeting events, with a definable cause that can be prevented or removed, are special-causes. Deming asserts common-cause variation accounts for 94% of variation. Only management can work on the process to reduce common-cause variation: they cannot blame the workers, and cannot assign "belts" to reduce it for them.
While all things have causes, responding to random variation as if it had a discrete cause leads to ever increasing error. Two mistakes must happen when managing variation:
1. To react to an outcome as if it came from a special-cause, when actually it came from common cause variation.
2. To react to an outcome as if it came from common-cause variation, when it actually came from a special-cause.

Control charts provide the tool to minimize both mistakes.
LPM/CCPM uses buffers to manage common-cause variation, and project risk management to help control special-causes.

Deming's Experiments
Deming ran simple experiments to teach many elements of variation. Two of his 14 lessons from his **red bead** experiment, illustrating mistake 1 (p. 172-174) are:
1. Ranking of people is wrong because it primarily measures the effect of the system on people.
2. The futility of pay for performance.

Deming ran another simple experiment with a **funnel** to illustrate the mistakes one can make when not understanding variation. It graphically illustrated the effect of mistaking common-cause variation for special-cause, and thereby "tampering" with the system.

Deming, W. E. (1993). The New Economics. Cambridge, MA: MIT Press

Control Charts
Control charts determine if your project delivery system is stable, guide action to operate the process, and improve it over time. Module 9.3 suggests basic control charts for your project delivery (LPM/CCPM) system and describes how to use them.

Wheeler, D. (2000). Understanding Variation. Knoxville, TN: SPC Press

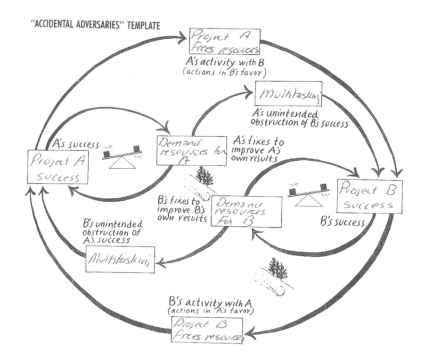

Causal Loop Diagram Archetype for "Accidental Adversaries": Vicious cycle. *Causal loop diagram illustrates the connections and influence directions. The example shows projects competing for resources: that is, a lack of project priority causes rampant multitasking, so both projects lose. The snowballs illustrate positive reinforcing feedback loops; the scales indicate negative balancing loops (after Senge et. al. 1994, p. 147)*

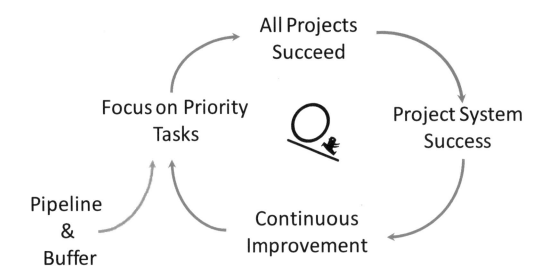

The Three Rules and Continuous Improvement Change the System to a Virtuous Cycle.

3.4.3 Appreciation for A System

Purpose   Effective system operation and ongoing improvement requires effective system design with ongoing improvement processes built in.

System   A system is a "*network of interdependent components that work together to try to accomplish the aim of the system*". Project delivery systems are dynamic and non-linear, which means their behavior is complex. They are controlled by many feedback loops, which make predictability difficult. Peter Senge posed a set of non-intuitive "laws" for such systems:

1. *There are no right answers.*
2. *You can't divide the elephant in half.*
3. *Cause and effect are not closely related in time and space.*
4. *You can have your cake and eat it too: but not all at once.*
5. *The easiest way out leads back in.*
6. *Behavior will grow worse before it grows better.*

It will take some study of the references for these to make sense to you.

Senge et. al. note, "Changing the way we interact means redesigning not just the formal structures of the organization, but the hard-to-see patterns of interaction between people and processes" (p. 48).

This book concerns the project delivery system depicted in module 5.1: everything from project selection to satisfactory closure of projects. Most would agree to an aim of that system similar to: deliver defect-free project benefits to customers of the projects (may be internal users), in the shortest time, and for the least cost.

Senge, P. (1990). The Fifth Discipline. New York: Doubleday
Senge, P., Ross, R. et. al. (1884). The Fifth Discipline Field book. New York: Doubleday

Destruction of a System   Deming points out that many organizations design their structures to defeat the aim of the system. For example, as illustrated by the system diagram on the left, if each project manager competes for resources, workers will be harried, stressed, and usually driven to multitasking, which in turn causes errors and slows down all the projects. A vicious cycle of system destruction ensues. This system causal loop diagram should make it clear why the more detail direction of solution cannot help the system, even if it did improve the performance of each part of the system.

If you tried to build an automobile from "the best" of each part out there; engine from one type, transmission from another, and so on, it wouldn't work. Everyone doing his or her best does not make an effective system. More detail does not make projects flow to completion faster and better.

Managing the System   System thinking isn't hard, but sometimes is not intuitive. It requires the will to do it. The tools exist to effectively design and operate any type of business or government system. Leadership must understand system dynamics and design. Senior managers must have a mind-set that their primary job is to design and improve the system, not to tend to the day-to-day operation.

Applying the three rules, the LPM system, and continuous improvement creates a new system to reinforce a virtuous cycle of positive system performance and improvement as illustrated by the lower causal-loop system diagram.

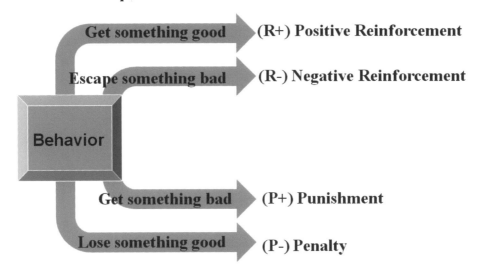

Consequences That INCREASE Behavior

Get something good → (R+) Positive Reinforcement

Escape something bad → (R-) Negative Reinforcement

Behavior

Get something bad → (P+) Punishment

Lose something good → (P-) Penalty

Consequences That DECREASE Behavior

Daniels, A. and Daniels, J. (2000). Performance Management, (p. 56)

Behavior Reinforcement Determines Its Repetition. *Changing the behavior in an organization requires decreasing undesired behavior and increasing desired behavior: starting with the most senior management!*

Results Measures
- Decide which behaviors to focus on
- Determine if behavior reinforcement is working as planned

Behavior Measures
- Feedback to performers
- Use to reinforce behavior

Start

Pinpoint **Results**

Pinpoint **Behaviors**

Measure

Feedback

Reinforce

Monitor & **Improve**

Measures Provide Valuable Tools to Elicit Desired Behaviors. *Measure both results and the behaviors that cause those results. Use the measurement feedback to provide reinforcement. See module 6.1.1.*

Psychology
Deming notes that, "Psychology helps us to understand people, interaction between people and circumstances, interaction between customer and supplier, interaction between teacher and pupil, interaction between a manager and any system of management" (p. 110). He then focuses on learning, motivation, and leadership. Gaining profound knowledge of psychology is a life-long pursuit.
Deming, W. E. (1993). The New Economics. Cambridge, MA: MIT Press, p. 94 ff.

Motivate
Deming's definition above focuses on interactions, because he observes that most managers exhibit what psychologists call the "fundamental attribution error"; i.e. blaming everything on the person nearest the outcome. He illustrates how results attributed to individual employees are actually from the interactions of the system and other people on the employee, and the consequences of natural variation. Management's response to "poor" results, and lack of reinforcing behaviors that cause desired results, usually works to decrease motivation over the tenure of most employees. The science of psychology and understanding of the system of variation make us able to do much better than that…starting with leadership.

Lead
I can do no better than quote the Tao Te Ching:

The best leaders are those the people hardly know exist.
The next best is a leader who is loved and praised.
Next comes the one who is feared.
The worst one is the leader that is despised.

If you don't trust the people,
They will become untrustworthy.

The best leaders value their words, and use them sparingly.
When she has accomplished her task,
The people say, "Amazing:
We did it, all by ourselves!"

Measure
Measures enable management by fact, and can be a source of management reinforcement for desired behaviors and to increase internal motivation. Measures must address both the results desired from the system, and the behavior necessary to produce those results. The behavior measures are most important because they provide the feedback necessary to enable reinforcement.
Daniels, A. and Daniels, J. (2006). Performance Management. Atlanta, GA: Performance Management Publications

Reinforce

Most people misunderstand the meaning of behavior consequence reinforcement. They equate it with tangible rewards: give the doggie another treat. While that actually works with animals, and even simpler human behaviors (e.g. gambling), people are more sophisticated, and the tangible rewards quickly cause unintended negative effects: they decrease intrinsic motivation. Kohn's studies demonstrate this in detail. Instead, reinforcement finds what works for the person involved, and helps them obtain it when the behavior supports the organizational system needs. See Nelson for ideas on intangibles. (He should have titled his book "Reinforcers".)
Kohn, A. (1993). Punished by Rewards. New York: Houghton Mifflin Company
Nelson, R. (1994). 1001 Ways to Reward Employees. Workman Publishing Company.

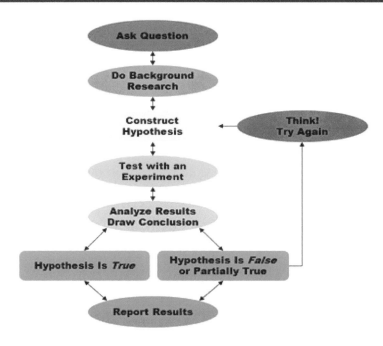

Scientific Method. *The primary points are test, test, and test.*

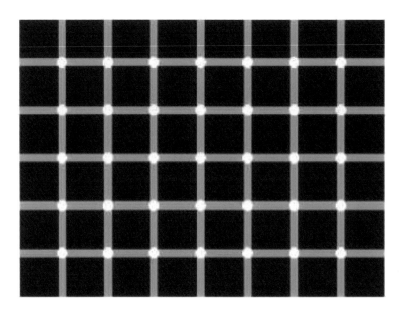

Belief-> Attention-> Perception-> Belief. *Count the black dots. Although this image preys on a "hardware" element of our visual perception, similar things happen when we seek to understand reality through our belief systems. That's why Deming stressed, "As a good rule, Profound Knowledge must come from the outside." (There are no black dots!)*

3.4.5 Theory of Knowledge

Purpose

Correct decisions and predictions require a theory of knowledge. A person needs a plan for how to get home, and that plan needs prediction.
Deming, W. E. (1993). The New Economics. Cambridge, MA: MIT Press, p. 94 ff.

No True Value

This can get pretty deep for most people. Quite a few people spend their lives discussing the Philosophy of Science. You do not have to be a philosopher to know enough for what Deming means by Profound Knowledge: but you do have to internalize a few non-intuitive ideas.

The first is that there is no "true value" to any characteristic, state, or condition defined in terms of measurement or observations. The idea that more detail ensures better accuracy is wrong. Indeed, the implied understanding of that idea is wrong: accuracy is the range of variation of results; it does not relate to a single "true value". Some suggest precision relates variation to a "true value", but that is also wrong. Precision can only relate the variation relative to a value obtained with an operational definition; i.e. a standard.

Scientific Method

The Scientific Method provides an enormous contribution to the growth of human knowledge. Before it, progress was slow and erratic. Since the scientific method, progress has increased exponentially. Many scientists think Karl Popper does the best job of describing the scientific method…at least how it should work. The first key to the scientific method confirms that there is no way to know a truth. The best we can do is to propose theories and subject them to critical discussion and rigorous falsification tests. We can test new theories vs. old, and pick the one that works best. No number of positive examples establishes a theory as valid. That's why non-sciences such as astrology always trot out true believers to state their positive case. Even if true, such positive statements say nothing about the theory.

The top figure illustrates Popper's hypothetico-deductive approach.

One consequence of this approach is that the idea of "induction" is fatally flawed. Only deduction works in reality.
Popper, K. (1979). Objective Knowledge. Oxford, UK: Oxford University Press

Predicted Effect

Goldratt emphasizes using predicted effects to test assertions about systems. It is a form of fallacy checking. Deming stressed, "A statement devoid of prediction or explanation of past events is of no help for the management of a system." Whenever you hear or read a theory, use prediction to test it for yourself. Ask, "If this were true, what would I expect to observe?" Then look for it. Systems in a state of statistical control provide the only rational basis for prediction. All other predictions are just guesses.

Predicted effect is a powerful tool when used with the PDSA or DMAIC cycle. Do small tests to determine if you get the desired effects and do not get irresolvable unintended consequences from any posed improvement. This includes LPM/CCPM!

Operational Definitions

Operational definitions offer a practical result from a theory of knowledge. Operational definitions give a precise procedure "which reasonable people can agree on and do business with" to measure something, and unambiguous decision rules to tell us how to act on the result obtained. Be sure to use them!

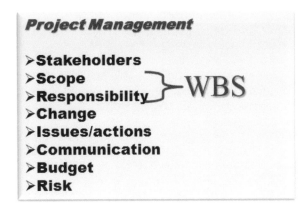

Project Management
- Stakeholders
- Scope ⎫
- Responsibility ⎬ WBS
- Change
- Issues/actions
- Communication
- Budget
- Risk

Critical Chain
- Schedule
  - Critical Chain
  - Buffers
  - Pipelining
- EXECUTION
  - Task dispatching
  - Status
  - Buffer management

CCPM Adds Key Elements of Professional Project Management to Critical Chain. *The items listed on the left indicate what I consider a minimal set for most project environments.*

Project Size

	Small	Large
Low (Project Risk)	**Simple Project Plan** -Charter -WBS (With Responsibility) -Budget (Spreadsheet) -Schedule (Resourced)	**Moderate** -Small Project Plan -WBS, Scope Statement, Work Packages -Integrated CSCS
High (Project Risk)	**Moderate** -Small Project Plan -Design & Peer Review -Risk Management Plan -Quality Plan	**Full Project Plan** -All Project Plan Elements -Supporting Plans -Procedures -Process Training -Project Controls Function

Professional Project Management Elements Scale to the Projects and Environment. *The full list of processes and procedures contemplated by the PMBOK™ Guide only apply to the largest and most complex project environments. This table provides a guide to scaling elements of a Project Plan.(CSCS = Cost Schedule Control System)*

CC+PM   I first defined the acronym CCPM (Critical Chain Project Management) at an International meeting of the Project Management Institute (PMI) in Long Beach, CA in 1997, and used the wording as the title to the first edition of my first book, published in 2000. I meant it to synthesize Dr. Goldratt's breakthrough ideas on critical chain with the necessary elements of the project management profession. The good news is that the acronym has been widely adopted. The bad news is that most use it to mean simply "critical chain scheduling", or worse yet is the 3rd edition of the PMBOK™ Guide mislabeled even critical chain as "a network analysis technique".

PM Key Elements   PMI's OPM3 and other maturity models such as the CMMI for software tend to equate the probability of success with the weight of the written procedures that guide project delivery. That direction is incorrect. We need to focus on the necessary conditions for project success in each environment and recognize that they vary widely. I have found a few to be necessary for most project environments, but that the comprehensive listings equate to trying to eat everything on the menu in a restaurant. It will not make you feel good. The figure illustrates the elements I consider key.

Project Schedules   Many people consider a schedule as a list of due dates. They call such lists "plans". Long before Goldratt invented critical chain, I found it useful to differentiate between schedules and Project Plans. I recall the posters we prepared to hang in all the office spaces of one huge project, "A schedule is not a Project Plan!" See module 5.7 for a Project Plan definition agreed to by the international body that formulates the PMBOK™ Guide.

That leaves us with schedules. A critical chain schedule is a schedule, even though it does not (externally) use individual task completion dates. Whenever anyone asks when a critical chain project task is scheduled to finish, there is always one answer: "as soon as possible after it starts". Critical chain project schedules provide dates for the start of chains that have no predecessors, including the project start date, and for the end of the project, which is the end of the project buffer. They can have dates for milestones, and can also have milestones representing phases or deliverables without dates. Whenever a milestone does have a date, it must have a buffer preceding it. All output dates from CCPM schedules have buffers as their predecessors.

Execution   I have come to believe that the PMBOK Guide underemphasizes execution. Although execution is one of the identified phases, it is not one of the knowledge areas. While each knowledge area has some element of execution, it is a small element and not connected to the degree that the planning elements are. Although the guide mentions variability, it is not as prominent as needs to be to aid project success.

Pipelining   Multiproject execution is unique to CCPM. Although PMI has come to recognize programs and portfolios of projects, their material does not yet embrace how to work during multiproject execution so as to enhance the overall flow of work. Although integrated "resource planning" applications such as SAP and PeopleSoft have come to recognize the need for it, they do not enable a solution such as pipelining or project management tools as effective as deployed for CPM and CCPM execution.

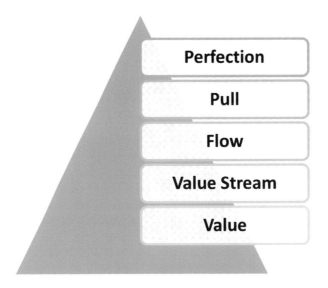

Womack and Jones's Emphasized Five Lean Principles. *A variety of Lean tools and perspectives such as visual control and single piece flow (synchronization) fall under these principles.*

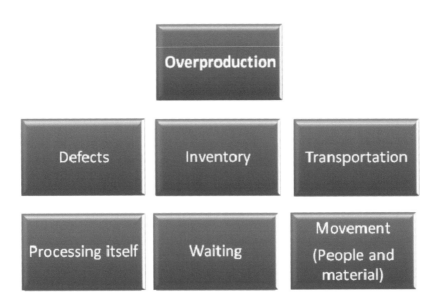

The Seven Basic Forms of Waste Start the Search for Improvement. *Shiego asserts that all organizations start with at least 83% waste (xvi).*

The Beginning Lean began with Taiichi Ohno's development of the Toyota Production System (TPS) starting in 1945. His principle objective was to "produce many models in small quantities" (p.2). By 1988, it had moved to "looking at the time line from the moment the customer gives us an order to the point when we collect the cash. And we are reducing that time line by removing non-value-added waste" (p. ix). Application of most of his ideas to projects is evident and powerful. Womack and Jones brought the Lean idea to the United States in the 1990s, focusing on five principles and seven wastes. Applications towards ever higher levels of perfection in all business work are just beginning.

Ohno, T. (1988). *Toyota Production System*: Beyond Large-scale Production. Portland, OR: Productivity Press.
Womack, J. and Jones, D. (1996). *Lean Thinking*. New York: Simon & Shuster

Principles Womack and Jones sought to organize Lean Thinking into the five principles listed in the graphic. Ohno and Shingo seem to focus more on the system and process, e.g. Shingo notes, "To make fundamental improvements in the production process, we must distinguish product flow (process) from work flow (operations) and analyze them separately" (p.4). Multiple perceptions enhance identification of opportunities to eliminate waste.

Shingo, S. (1989). *A Study of the Toyota Production System*. Portland, OR: Productivity Press

Waste Types Ohno notes, "the greatest waste of all is excess inventory" (p.54), "called the waste of overproduction" (p. 59). Project language usually does not address inventory, which I define for projects as "all of the work performed on projects that are not yet complete and producing their benefits". Project inventory directly affects project flow because new projects must wind their way through the pile of projects in progress. Shingo adds, "process consists of four components: processing, inspection, transport, and delay operations. Of these, only processing adds value; the others can be viewed as waste" (p. 77). This perspective relates all of the waste types to project tasks as processes.

Flow & Pull Flow and Pull are two sides of the same issue. Pulling projects into the system only as the system can process them enhances flow. Enhanced flow enables more pull. Womack and Jones note, "the general principle of doing one thing at a time and working on it continuously until completion applies to improvement activities with the same force that it applies to design, order-taking, and production activities" (p. 95).

Future The Lean literature refers to where the Japanese were 30 plus years ago. Where are they today? More importantly, where are they going? Shingo notes, "The critical point---and the one that takes the most time to ensure---- is that top management must have both a clear understanding of the issues and the zeal needed to carry through to the end" (p.224). We have to move beyond where *they* are going (not just get to where they have been or are) in order to create a unique competitive position in the global market.

4. Execute

Execute is not one of the nine areas of the Project Management Body of Knowledge. Although it is one of the phases described therein, the amount of guidance on execution is small compared to the amount devoted to planning. Although I learned to value Project Plans early in my career, and still value them, I have come to understand that effective execution is more important than the Project Plan. A moderately good Project Plan, effectively executed, will deliver success. A world class Project Plan, if not used in execution, will lead to a failed project.

I was fortunate to learn the key to successful work execution early in my career. I was promoted several supervisory levels quite rapidly. My workload grew with responsibility level. I knew that wasn't a good thing and that at some point you have to seriously learn to delegate. I put energy into that, and got pretty good at delegating. Yet, my work load was always waiting to fill all my available time. I started reading books on "Getting Things Done" (one of the better actual titles). Before long, I understood the key: focus on one task at a time. There was only one problem: "Which task?"

About that time, several of my employees began showing up at meetings with a nice little binder, in which I saw them taking their notes. I asked one of them what it was, and she explained it was a Franklin Planner™. It looked like many others, such as a Day-Timer®, but, I was assured, the secret was in the system. Further inquiry revealed that there was a low cost class available to learn how to use it. I signed up immediately. What I found impressed me so much I use it today, over thirty years later. I also made the training and binder available to anyone in my organization (about 600 people at the time) who was interested. There was no pushing it; we just said, "If you want to go, Larry will approve having the company pay for it." Within a month, over 80% of the people in the organization had attended! It was remarkable all the more because we had taken over a year, with constant pushing, to get a smaller percentage through some required training on quality improvement.

Organization performance improved dramatically and immediately, and sustained the improved level through the rest of my time there. The secret was focus on one task at a time. But in order to focus on one task at a time, people needed a tool and a priority process. The priority process we used at that time was the one put forth by what is now Franklin-Covey: first ranking tasks in accordance with their importance (A, B, C), and then ranking them sequentially based on their urgency (1,2,3...). The process worked as well for me as an individual as it did for the organization as a whole.

Now, with LPM/CCPM, we have a better way to plan for and prioritize the project tasks. But everyone also has some degree of non-project tasks. The secret to productivity remains the same: focus.

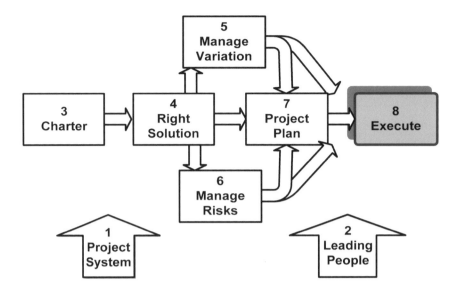

Lean Project Management Focus on Execution Flows from Plans to Project Completion

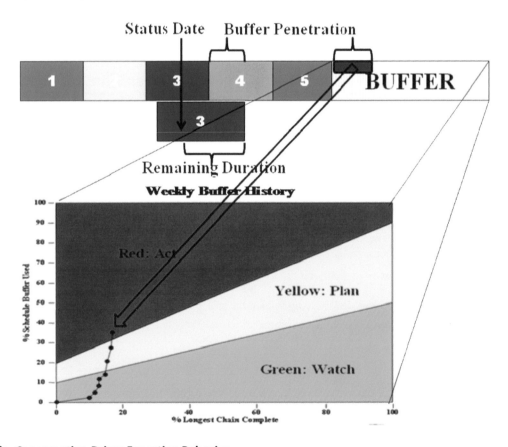

Buffer Consumption Drives Execution Behavior

4.1 Focus on Execution

Overall

Unlike complex project management approaches that drive excruciating detail, Lean Project Management (LPM) focuses on project execution. Execution focus requires effective plans and some non-intuitive behaviors from all project stakeholders. LPM uses critical chain plans to enable all resources to focus on the right tasks and perform them the right way.

Buffer Management

Buffers, the unique element of CCPM, provide the means for effective execution. Status of critical chain plans enables a measure of the amount of buffer consumed as the project progresses. The fever chart plots the maximum amount of buffer consumed by the project tasks vs. progress made along the critical chain. Predetermined criteria on the fever chart tell the project team when to plan for and initiate buffer recovery. The task causing the largest buffer use (consumption or penetration) pinpoints where to focus buffer recovery.

The Right Tasks

Buffer use guides resources to focus on the right task. Effective buffer management predicts the impact each task has on the project buffer. Resources work on the task using the most buffer penetration.

The Right Way

Project flow demands that resources focus on one task at a time, completing it before going back to their task list to find out which task to work on next. Focus on one task at a time, like a relay racer focusing on running their part of the race, greatly reduces task duration and quality defects. Task managers, usually the first level supervisors, focus on helping task resources overcome obstacles to performing as a relay racer; e.g. expediting necessary task inputs.

Behavior

Management behavior determines LPM success. Management must reinforce organization behaviors that enable project flow. Management must:
> - Minimize the Work in Process (WIP) with project pipelining.
> - Ensure effective project plans with appropriate buffers.
> - Establish and use the LPM measures to determine when and where to help task managers recover buffer.
> - Reinforce relay-racer task performance.

Non-intuitive

Certain LPM behaviors are not intuitive to most people:
> - Add buffers to reduce project duration.
> - Delay the start of projects to complete them sooner.
> - Delay starting work on tasks to complete more tasks quicker and with higher quality.
> - Reduce the number of projects worked on at one time to increase the number of projects complete over time (Throughput).

Results demonstrate that applying these non-intuitive behaviors to execution causes the LPM benefits.

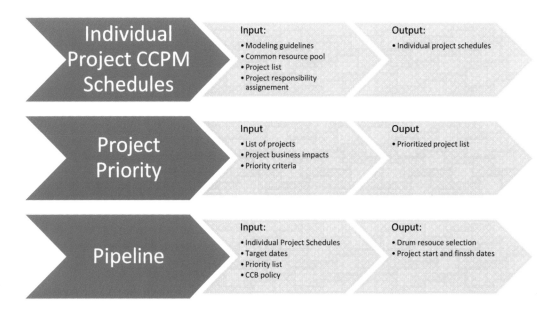

Individual Project CCPM Schedules

Input:
- Modeling guidelines
- Common resource pool
- Project list
- Project responsibility assignement

Output:
- Individual project schedules

Project Priority

Input:
- List of projects
- Project business impacts
- Priority criteria

Ouput:
- Prioritized project list

Pipeline

Input:
- Individual Project Schedules
- Target dates
- Priority list
- CCB policy

Ouput:
- Drum resouce selection
- Project start and finssh dates

Pipelining Process Starts with Individual Project Schedules *Initial project schedules are built with an arbitrary start date, usually the date of starting the network. The pipelining process outputs project start and finish dates.*

The Pipeline Module 2.4 illustrates the most common approach to pipelining; visualizing the project demand as filling a time graph, and moving projects so that the maximum demand for the drum resource does not exceed the effective supply; i.e. the actual supply minus the CCB allowance. Module 4.2.2 illustrates another view, with the CCB between projects, connecting the use of the drum on one project to its use on the next project in the pipeline. The latter view only works for the simplest cases of a few small projects with only a few tasks using the drum resource, and a few units of the drum resource (usually only one).

In some cases, a very simple pipelining approach may be feasible, such as only starting a new project when a project completes. Such cases entail a number of assumptions that you must assure continue to be met over time.

Process Pipelining is a process, not a one-time event. New projects continuously enter the system, and projects will leave the system as they complete. The process should be transparent and non-intrusive to the ongoing flow of work. In normal circumstances, the addition of new projects should not affect the progress of ongoing projects. Pipelining often entails setting up and evaluating a number of "what if" cases. A Master Scheduler normally owns the pipelining process.

Target Dates Projects often have target dates. Such dates may be determined by contract, regulation, or other factors. Project priority should reflect target dates, and the pipeline should be adjusted as necessary to maximize accommodating target dates.

Multiple Pipelines Larger organizations may maintain multiple pipelines. This makes sense when groups of projects (portfolios) cannot share resources; e.g. because of physical locations or types of projects.

Controlling WIP Pipelining controls the number of projects in work at any time (WIP: Work in Progress or Process). This reduces the pressure to multitask and eliminates chaos in many organizations. Little's law, a queuing theory relationship between cycle time and work in progress, ensures that reducing work in progress reduces overall project duration (cycle time).

Capacity Constraint Buffer (CCB) Policy Module 8.3.1 recommends that individual project schedules use a single simple work calendar and assumes resources are available 100% of the time; e.g. Monday to Friday, 8 -5, with a 40-hour work week, and include only holidays taken by all employees. In this context, the CCB must serve two purposes:

1. Minimize queues for the drum resource.
2. Account for non-productive time of the drum resource.

The first purpose demands a minimum size representing about 25% of the drum supply. Most organizations provide for vacation, sick days, training time, etc. yielding productive annual person-hours on the order of 1,600, as compared to 2,000 with only holidays removed. This suggests the capacity constraint buffer should include 20% for the second purpose, for a total of 45% of the available resource. Thus, if the drum resource comprised ten individuals, projects should be pipelined assuming six resources. Note that individual project tasks must also not exceed six resources for this to work.

4.2.1 Flow-focused Project Schedules

LPM/CCPM Schedule	CPM Schedule

•WBS for Deliverables
•Task Flow:
  •Finish-to start relationships only,
  •No lead-lags
•Task represents hand-off:
  •Between resources (pass baton)
  •Necessary detail contained in checklists
•Limited task detail (~ 300 tasks max per schedule)
•Single project end milestone
•Internal undated milestones
•Critical chain: longest chain through network consdering both:
  •Task relationships
  •Resource demand and supply
•Buffered milestone dates
•Synchronization via. feeding buffers
•Resource leveled
•Project buffer determines project completion date
	•WBS for Deliverables
	•Task date detail:
	  • Various relationships
	  • Lead-lags
	•Task start and finish dates
	•Task represents work detail
	•Unlimited detail
	•Critical path
	  •Not longest path if not resource-leveled
	  •Often no reasonable solution after resource leveling
	•Common mistakes:
	  •No critical path identified
	  •Tasks with no successors
	  •Links to summary task

Flow-focused Project Schedules Guide Project Execution. *They do not schedule individual task start and completion dates because the actual duration necessary to perform project tasks varies.*

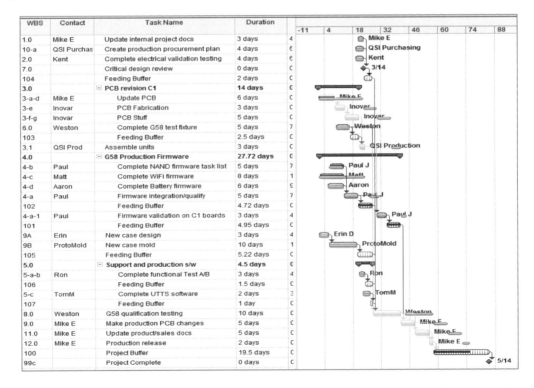

Example CCPM Schedule Shows Key Features. Critical chain tasks are lime colored. The magenta bars are "likely start and finish" for incomplete tasks...updated from task status.

4.2.1 Flow-focused Project Schedules

Flow Focus

LPM/CCPM schedules focus on the flow of the work. Consider the schedule as a roadmap of the work necessary to deliver the project result. Although scheduling programs use dates on all tasks for calculation purposes, most individual task dates have no meaning in LPM/CCPM schedules. Only the start dates for chains and buffered completion dates matter. Eliminating the focus on task dates greatly simplifies developing and maintaining schedules.

Detail

Because LPM/CCPM schedules primarily guide the handoff of work from one resource to another they require much less detail than is commonly used in Critical Path Method (CPM) schedules. If additional work detail is necessary for a given task that information is supplied by other than the schedule, e.g. checklists. LPM/CCPM networks commonly reduce network size (number of tasks) and complexity (number of relationships) by a factor of ten.

The general guidance for task detail in LPM/CCPM schedules is that tasks should range from no less than 2% to less than 10% of the duration of the critical chain. The reason for the minimum limit is to prevent excessive detail in the plans. The reason for the maximum limit is to enable effective control, in view of task variability. A single large task overrun cannot be allowed to cause a project to be late; there must be opportunity to recover buffer.

Relationships and Constraints

Because the purpose of the LPM/CCPM schedule is to guide resources to work on the right tasks and hand-off to other resources, the links need only identify the hand offs; i.e. LPM/CCPM schedules use only finish-to-start links. The other relationships allowed in most scheduling programs and the many potential task constraints are not necessary. Most LPM/CCPM software enables the "Start No Earlier Than" (SNET) relationship to handle transactions with suppliers and external performers.

LPM/CCPM schedules can use two kinds of milestones: those with dates, and those without dates. Most milestones represent completion of deliverables, and thus do not have a date. When milestone dates are needed, they must always be buffered.

Other than the project start date, all dates of LPM/CCPM schedules must have buffers in front of them and must be outputs of the schedule tool. When need dates exist for the project result, the project schedule must be adjusted by logical and resource changes as necessary to achieve the desired date as an output of the schedule. Fixed dates on tasks prohibit determining the critical chain.

See section 8 for more detail on creating LPM/CCPM networks.

Handoffs

Task boundaries are usually when one primary resource hands off the task result to another primary resource. You should override this rule if it leads to task durations that significantly exceed the recommended maximum task duration; i.e. 10% of the critical chain. In those cases, tasks must be divided to represent intermediate deliverables that can be clearly statused as complete.

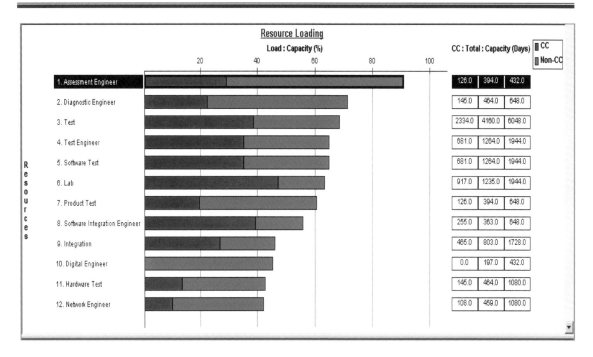

Use Projected Resource Load vs. Capacity to Select the Drum. *The drum should be a highly loaded resource that is not easy to increase, and is in a quantity larger than one, such as the Assessment Engineer resource shown above. Opinions vary as to whether you should choose a resource used on more or less percent of critical chain tasks. This figure is from the Concerto software.*

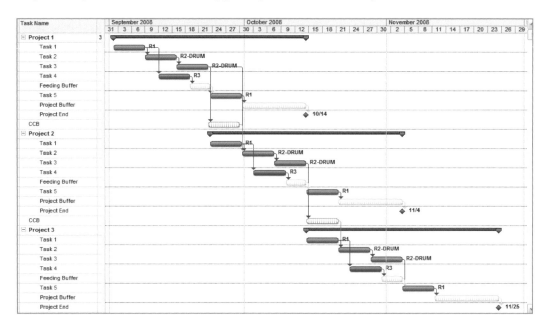

Pipelining Moves Whole Projects to Not Overload the Drum (R2). *The schedules for non-drum resources can exhibit temporary overloads (e.g. R1). The overloads may not occur in reality and can be absorbed by buffers.*

Drum

The drum controls the start of projects. The name comes from the TOC approach to production, evoking the image of a drumbeat setting the pace for work. The drum sets the start date for projects. Initially referred to as "staggering" of projects, most now call this release of projects for work **_Pipelining_**. Pipelining evokes the idea of flowing projects through a constrained capacity…the pipe. The drum is a system concept. It has no meaning to individual projects. Larger organizations can deploy different drums for project portfolios if the portfolios do not share resources.

Drum Selection

The initial and usual approach for the drum uses a resource highly loaded relative to its capacity. Although ideally it would be the most highly loaded resource, estimates of resource demand entail significant uncertainty, causing uncertain selection. The good news is that it usually doesn't matter. If the drum selection provides an appropriate control on the amount of work in progress to help eliminate multitasking pressure and enable projects to complete within the project buffer, then the selected drum resource can be good enough, even if not THE most highly loaded. The selected resource should not be easy or cheap to increase; e.g. it should be skilled staff vs. unskilled staff, or an expensive and/or long-lead facility or machine.

Note that the drum resource need not be a human resource. For example, it may be a test facility that all project results must use, and that has limited capacity. In this case, you can treat the resource the same way you would treat a human resource; i.e. load a resource named "test facility" on the appropriate tasks, with as many units of parallel capacity as the supply of that resource.

Alternative

Please do not make the mistake of choosing an alternative approach for the drum until you have ensured that the resource-constraint approach is not the correct one for you. Alternatives have been developed for special cases; e.g. when and organization can support only a limited number of tasks of a given type, even though not specifically limited by resources to do so. For example, an IT organization may be able to support only a limited number of projects undergoing integration and user test at the same time. Thus, the drum may be a type of task, or even a project phase, vs. a specific resource. These alternatives come with significant assumptions which can be forgotten and thus used incorrectly. Nonetheless, one can use the same pipelining approach, by assigning a "virtual resource" to the task or tasks in the phase, and then pipelining to that virtual resource. Some, mistakenly in my opinion, call this a "virtual drum".

Changing Drums

Many organizations will find that the appropriate drum changes from time to time because of changes in the mix of project resource demand. You should verify the drum selection from time to time on a frequency equivalent to the rate at which your project mix changes; e.g. quarterly or annually. When the drum changes, it is necessary to adjust the pipeline for all incomplete projects. Started projects should be able to complete on time or earlier when the drum changes.

Pipelining

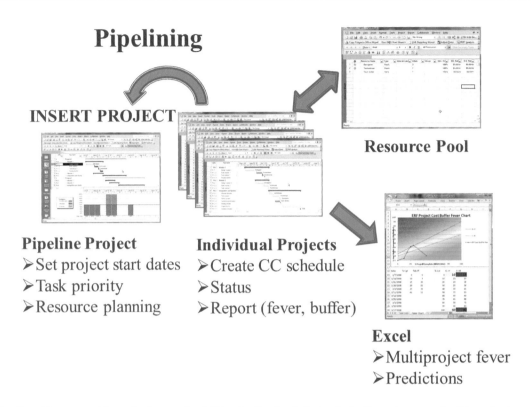

INSERT PROJECT

Resource Pool

Pipeline Project
➤ Set project start dates
➤ Task priority
➤ Resource planning

Individual Projects
➤ Create CC schedule
➤ Status
➤ Report (fever, buffer)

Excel
➤ Multiproject fever
➤ Predictions

Pipeline Process Uses Independent Single Project Schedule Development. *All projects must use a single resource pool.*

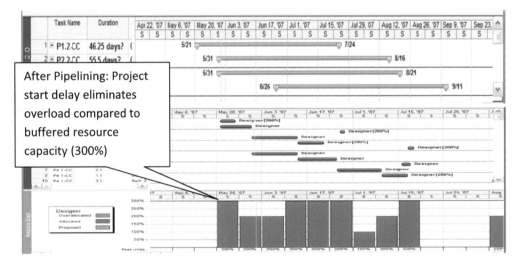

Pipelining Delays the Start of Projects to Allow for a Capacity Constraint Buffer for the Drum Resource. *The capacity constraint buffer accounts for all resource demands, including non-productive time, and provides protective capacity to minimize task delay. For this case, four resources (400%) are available, allowing a 25% CCB.*

Pipeline Purpose

Pipelining projects avoids overloading the drum resource. This provides necessary protective capacity for all less loaded resources.

Approach

Pipelining provides an operational tool that recognizes the variation in actual task duration. Unlike most enterprise scheduling methods, pipelining does not seek to level all resources across all projects. Pipelining allows even the drum resource to be overloaded for short periods of time in the initial planning. But since pipelining provides an adequate capacity constraint buffer for the most loaded resource, lesser loaded resources will have sufficient time to do their work. Sometimes temporary resource overloads will cause buffer penetration on one project while the resource focuses on a task on another project.

Pipeline Procedure

The procedure for pipelining:
1. Inserts all of the projects to be pipelined into the Pipeline Project (the Master Project) in priority order,
2. Selects the resource to use as the "drum" resource, and
3. Adjusts the start dates of the projects to level the load for only that resource, while allowing for a capacity constraint buffer.

One method to allow for the capacity constraint buffer is to put in a pseudo project that is one long task, loaded with the drum resource to the amount needed to represent the capacity constraint buffer. Then the total resource loading for the Master Project includes the capacity constraint buffer. Multiproject critical chain tools provide for the capacity constraint buffer in alternative ways.

Capacity Constraint Buffer

Size the ***capacity constraint buffer*** to ensure that the drum can process all work with minimal queue build-up. Plan individual projects assuming 100% resource availability to a common work calendar. Size the capacity constraint buffer to account for:
➢ Minimizing task queues (at least 25% of drum time)
➢ Non-productive time; e.g.
  o Vacation,
  o Sick leave,
  o Other high priority interrupt work (e.g. field problems), and
  o Training and other administrative time.
The capacity constraint buffer does not appear in a project plan, but is used at the organizational level to set the start date for projects.

Freeze Projects?

Dr. Goldratt's Strategy and Tactics (S&T) tree approach for the initial implementation of critical chain recommends freezing (i.e. stopping work) on 25% of projects to help eliminate multitasking and to flush excess Work in Progress (WIP) from the system. Creating the pipeline and implementing task dispatching implicitly accomplishes the same purpose for projects. It is often necessary to temporarily stop work on non-project tasks, and provide an ongoing process to prioritize non-project work as well to reduce initial WIP.

Maintain the Pipeline

Pipelining is an ongoing process. Management assigns one person, often called the "Master Scheduler", to maintain the pipeline. The Master Scheduler removes projects from the pipeline as they complete, and adds new projects as they arise. New projects can only enter the system through the pipeline. The Master Scheduler performs "What if?" analyses, to determine a preferred solution to match the organization performance capability to the work demands.

Resources Perform Work

Task Managers Dispatch and Status Tasks

Project Manager Leads Flow of Work

Project Team Manages Buffers

Resource Managers Provide Skilled Resources

Senior Managers Control WIP and Clear Roadblocks

Execution Enables Error-Free Focused Work on the Right Tasks. *Buffer penetration drives all execution actions.*

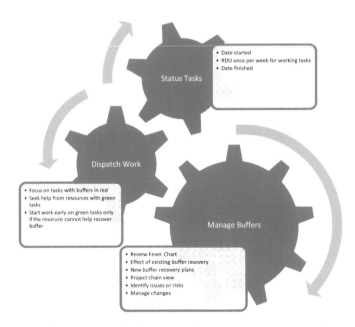

Status Tasks
- Date started
- RDU once per week for working tasks
- Date finished

Dispatch Work
- Focus on tasks with buffers in red
- Seek help from resources with green tasks
- Start work early on green tasks only if the resoruce cannot help recover buffer

Manage Buffers
- Review Fever Chart
- Effect of existing buffer resovery
- New buffer recovery plans
- Project chain view
- Identify issues or risks
- Manage changes

Execution Process. *Focus on the flow of work: forward actions necessary to complete the project as soon as possible.*

Execute

Leadership of LPM/CCPM project execution creates the difference. Although **Buffer Management** is a unique feature of LPM/CCPM project execution, key execution behaviors include:

1. Leadership:
   a. Setting the climate to enable relay-racer task performance
   b. Engaging to unstick work that is stuck for any reason, and to enable buffer recovery
2. Task Managers:
   a. Dispatching work to resources using prioritized task lists
   b. Statusing work using remaining duration, or "RDU"
3. Resource performing work using the relay-racer model
4. Project Managers:
   a. Planning and excuting buffer recovery
   b. Conducting effective buffer management meetings
   c. Acquiring data for continuous process improvement

Effective execution of the individual projects also requires management implementing key system processes, including: avoiding changing priorities or interruption of ongoing work, prioritizing projects, supporting effective buffer policies, pipelining to control WIP, and change management.

Management Role

Management acts as the project team's coach, mentor, and problem solver. Management performs actions escalated to them by project teams, wherever and whenever help is needed to unstick tasks or perform buffer recovery. Many task managers hold short (5 min) daily meetings with their team to assign tasks and receive escalated assistance requests.

Dispatch Work

Task managers dispatch work to resources in accordance with the buffer-status-driven task priority list by resource. When tasks get stuck, management should focus on helping to do whatever is necessary to get the work flowing. Although non-working tasks will move to higher in priority than working tasks, resources should complete a task once started and then go to the priority list to select the next task to work.

Status

Execution requires current task status. Tasks are in one of three modes:

1. Not started
2. In Work
3. Complete

Task managers status tasks:

1. Whenever a task starts
2. For ongoing tasks, at the working task status time (usually once per week, but can be more often)
3. Whenever a task completes

Status of ongoing work requires estimating remaining duration (RDU): the estimated number of full working days needed to complete the task.

Buffer Management

Buffer management consists of the two elements:

1. Dispatching work in accordance with buffer-driven task priority
2. Buffer recovery

Buffer recovery actions stem from the signals on the fever chart and the indicated task causing the most project buffer penetration.

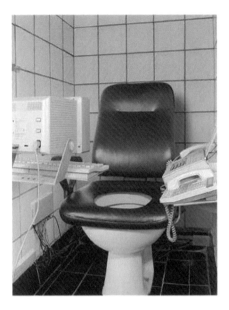

If You Feel Like You Need One of These, You Really Need This Module!

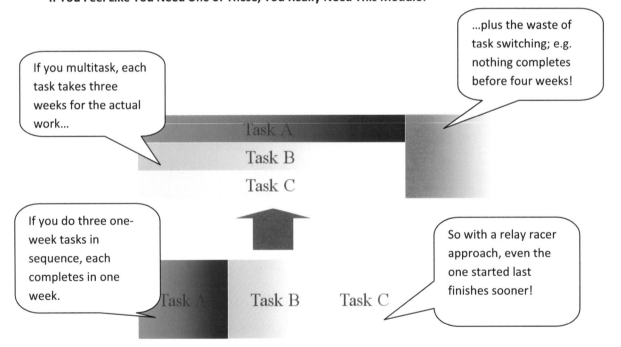

Multitasking Causes Direct and Indirect Waste. *The most immediate direct waste is on project duration, causing the extension of time until project benefits (e.g. cash) return to company, and the quality and productivity loss waste from task switching.*

Overall

Most organizations and projects are seriously afflicted with bad multitasking: multitasking that causes project tasks to take longer. Management causes multitasking, so management must change what they do first to flush it out of the organization. Multitasking can happen with individual workers and with groups of workers where more than one worker could contribute to a task.

Relay Racer Task Performance

Resources work on project tasks as if they were runners in an Olympic relay race. They position themselves to get the baton from their predecessor as early and smoothly as possible, focus 100% on completing their task as quickly as possible, and pass on the baton as early and smoothly as possible to the next racer.

Direct Waste

Multitasking causes the following direct wastes, which impact project duration (cycle time), throughput, quality, and productivity:

➢ Direct effect of switching between uncompleted tasks extends the duration of each task by the number of tasks

➢ The direct effect of lost time each time a task switch is made. Studies show switching attention on intellectual tasks can easily waste up to 40% of work time, and take at least 15 minutes per task switch (This includes allowing your phone, email, etc. to interrupt you!)

➢ Quality defects: studies demonstrate twice as many defects with task switching

Indirect Waste

Multitasking also causes waste indirectly:

➢ The effort necessary to correct the quality defects

➢ Lack of task synchronization

➢ Increasing queues of tasks to be worked on, causing

➢ Stress, which leads to lower and lower productivity, and more and more quality defects

The Right Task to Work On

Resources focus on the task causing the largest amount of buffer penetration. Task managers and supervisors consult the prioritized task list each time a task completes to find out which task to work on next. Task priority can change each time anyone statuses a contributing schedule. Ensure that everyone understands that once a task starts it should work to completion even though the priority list changes.

Supervisor and Middle Management Role

Supervisors and middle managers hold the keys to eliminating multitasking across the organization. Resources will work in the way management reinforces. Management must measure behavior feedback on multitasking and reinforce eliminating it. Supervisors take on the primary role of helping resources avoid multitasking by assisting them in task selection and frequent follow-up to determine where they can remove barriers to completing the task in hand. The most effective supervisors meet daily with their resources to determine where anyone is stuck and needs help, and they immediately solicit help from other managers where needed to ensure task synchronization, decision making, and clearing of obstacles.

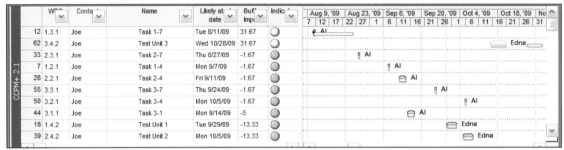

	WBS	Conta	Name	Likely st date	Buf Imp	Indic
12	1.3.1	Joe	Task 1-7	Tue 8/11/09	31.67	○
62	3.4.2	Joe	Test Unit 3	Wed 10/28/09	31.67	○
33	2.3.1	Joe	Task 2-7	Thu 8/27/09	-1.67	○
7	1.2.1	Joe	Task 1-4	Mon 9/7/09	-1.67	○
28	2.2.1	Joe	Task 2-4	Fri 9/11/09	-1.67	○
55	3.3.1	Joe	Task 3-7	Thu 9/24/09	-1.67	○
50	3.2.1	Joe	Task 3-4	Mon 10/5/09	-1.67	○
44	3.1.1	Joe	Task 3-1	Mon 9/14/09	-5	○
18	1.4.2	Joe	Test Unit 1	Tue 9/29/09	-13.33	○
39	2.4.2	Joe	Test Unit 2	Mon 10/5/09	-13.33	○

Task Manager (Contact Column) View Supports Task Dispatching. *Filter tasks by task manager, and then sort by buffer impact and start date for a given look-ahead period. Higher buffer impact = higher task priority…but not necessarily the task order. In this case, task 3.4.2 will have to wait on successor completion.*

➢ **Project Work**
   • Task managers control active WIP by assuring resources work one task at a time to the prioritized task lists
   • Projects are scheduled and Pipelined to project priority
   • Queued WIP includes only tasks ready-to-start (People cannot work on non-pipelined projects)
   • Active WIP should approach one task per resource, or less
   • Effective buffer management
   • Effective task escalation

➢ **Non-project Work**
   • Resources work one task at a time
   • Senior management sets general priority rules and prompt resolution of escalated decisions
   • Non-project tasks can be worked by resources with no red project tasks ready to work
   • Priority determined by supervisor (Task Manager)
   • Interruption of red tasks, or starting a non-project task when the resources is needed on a red project task, required senior management approval

Task Managers Must Have Rules to Integrate non-Project Work with Project Work. *Example.*

Purpose

Task managers dispatch work to performing resources according to the buffer status of candidate tasks to be worked. This achieves the highest organizational throughput. Task managers should apply local real-time knowledge to task assignments as they come up; e.g. who is sick, who can best work which available task, etc.

Resource Assignment

Most organizations should assign resource skills to tasks in the project schedule in accordance with a common resource skills list. Each task must also have a Task Manager by name. The task manager is accountable to complete the task work regardless of the actual resource situation when the task comes up for work. Task Managers are nominally first line supervisors with a number of resources available to them. They should apply their knowledge of the task, the resources, and resource availability relative to demand to assign a person to the task for execution. Generally the person assigned should focus on that task until it is complete.

There can be exceptions allowing resource assignment to task by name, for example where only one individual has the required skills, or for small projects in small organizations, where there is generally only one person with the necessary skills.

The general rule for assigning a person to a task is to assign the next available skilled person to the task causing the largest amount of buffer penetration. The task priority list, illustrated by the figure, enables such resource assignment to tasks.

Note that when a task is being worked, its buffer impact should stay the same or improve, while tasks not being worked will continue to impact the buffer. That is, the priority of non-working tasks tends to increase. This should not cause switching a resource from one task to another. Once a task is started, it should be completed in almost all cases, before the resource switches to another task.

Priority Interruptions

From time to time a resource working on a project task may be required to perform a higher priority non-project task. Normally this is a consequence of a field problem with product that only that resource can handle or a dire need on a high priority project; e.g. something breaks or a need for rework is discovered. Even in those cases the resource should generally be allowed to complete the working task and then switch to focus 100% to the priority task until it is done. If that does not work (e.g. substantial duration remains to complete the working task) be sure to put the working task into an easily recoverable state before turning away from it.

Task Escalation

Resources can get stuck on a task, i.e. unable to progress the task, for a variety of reasons. Unavailable inputs, including information or material from other tasks or decisions by management are the most frequent cause. The performing resource may run into an unknown situation they are not able to deal with by themselves. Or, they may run into a situation that requires help or decisions by others, and not be in a position to request the necessary input in a way that will ensure a response. Whatever the reason, the task manager must help the performing resource when this causes the task buffer impact to move into the yellow region.

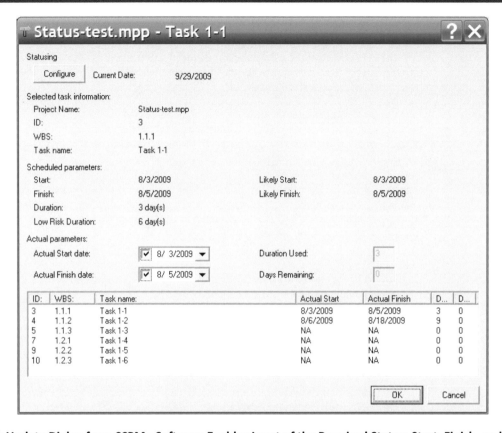

Task Update Dialog from CCPM+ Software Enables Input of the Required Status: Start, Finish, and Days Remaining (RDU).

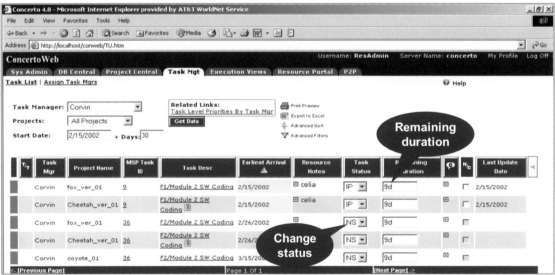

Concerto Software Input Screen Enables Additional Features, Such as Notes and Highlighting of Tasks With Completed Predecessors. *This example is produced by the Concerto software, used with permission of Realization Inc.*

Purpose

Task status provides the information necessary to make decisions on:
1. Which task to work on next
2. When and where management needs to help recover buffer

Management can only make correct decisions if all work is statused accurately and at the appropriate frequency for the set of projects.

Status

Tasks can be in three states:
1. Not started
2. Working
3. Complete

Correspondingly, task status must be input by the task manager:
1. When a task starts (actual date)
2. When a task finishes (actual date)
3. For tasks working at the regular status time (usually at the end of a given work day of the week), with an estimate of remaining duration (RDU)

Task managers estimate RDU; usually in working-days, based on their knowledge and experience of the situation with the task. If the RDU estimate would add a substantial amount to buffer penetration (e.g. more than about twice the original task duration estimate and larger than about 10% of the buffer) the task manager should provide an explanation of the cause and request escalation if help is necessary to unstick the task.

Standard Update Frequency

The standard task update frequency considers the overall length of projects and tasks. The standard task update frequency should be on the order of average task duration; e.g. daily if tasks are on the average a day or less and weekly if tasks on are on the order of a week or more. For short projects with task durations less than one day it may be necessary to have the standard update frequency every shift. Generally the standard task update frequency should not exceed weekly or the project will lose a sense of urgency. It is helpful to couple the standard update with another routine action; e.g. weekly time reporting, as this can help trigger the required action. In organizations with short task durations, some task managers do the update following routine early-shift "stand up meetings" where they also dispatch tasks.

Why Remaining Duration?

The practice of statusing critical chain schedules with RDU (in contrast to % complete as used in many CPM software tools) has three purposes:
1. More accurate estimate of buffer penetration because it forces the task managers to think about the remaining things required to complete the task.
2. Estimate in the units needed to directly know the effect on buffer penetration.
3. The ability to communicate delays that will extend beyond the original estimated task duration.

The third point is most significant, because it provides a simple vehicle to alert management when something has occurred on a task that may require management action. % complete only allows projecting the task completion forward by the amount of the original task duration estimate, by putting in 0% complete. RDU does not suffer from this unnecessary and dangerous limitation.

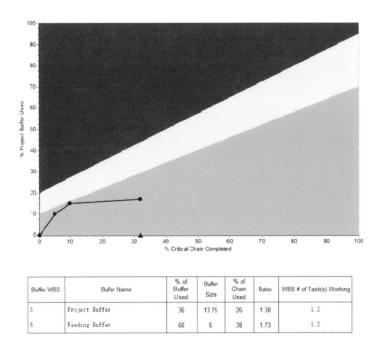

Buffer WBS	Buffer Name	% of Buffer Used	Buffer Size	% of Chain Used	Ratio	WBS # of Task(s) Working
5	Project Buffer	36	13.75	26	1.38	1, 2
6	Feeding Buffer	66	6	38	1.73	1, 2

Start Buffer Meetings With Fever Chart. *Buffer penetration drives all execution actions.*

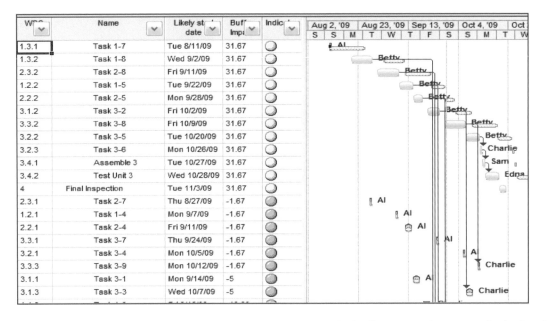

Project Chain View Focuses Buffer Recovery. *Tasks are grouped by buffer impact for a given look-ahead period. Tasks with the same amount of buffer penetration are normally on the same chain, providing the next candidates for buffer recovery.*

4.3.4 Buffer Meetings

Purpose
Buffer meetings have a single purpose: to move the project to complete as soon as possible. They should be short and focused. They should provide top-level project communication that must be shared by all, and conclude with specific actions to move the project forward.

Agenda
Set a standard time, place, and agenda for buffer meetings. The buffer meeting should immediately follow your standard project status update. Actions from the meeting must be communicated to all project stakeholders. Your agenda should be something like the following:
1. Review of fever chart: trends, tasks causing buffer penetration
   a. Assess effectiveness of in-process buffer recovery actions
2. Review statused critical chain Gantt chart to look ahead and solicit issues
3. Review the Project Chain View (see graphic) to assign actions for buffer recovery when and where needed
4. Verify progress on previously assigned actions
5. Communicate approved project changes
6. Review project risk list:
   a. Risks that are occurring (ensure action)
   b. Risks to add
   c. Risks to delete
7. Summarize new actions
8. Conclude with information items

Task managers of stuck tasks and tasks in the yellow or red must attend buffer management meetings. Attendance by others can be flexible.

Buffer Recovery
Assign buffer recovery action to one person to lead: normally the task manager for the task causing maximum buffer penetration. Sometimes you may prefer to assign someone else to lead buffer recovery if the working task manager is fully occupied getting the task unstuck or does not have adequate knowledge of downstream task candidates for buffer recovery. Buffer recovery actions should be written and communicated to the whole team. Assign buffer recovery planning when the task buffer impact is in the yellow and ensure that the plans activate when the buffer impact moves into the red region.

Project Chain View
The Project Chain View provides the primary tool for the buffer management meeting. You can reproduce the key functionality of the project chain view with most project scheduling software or by exporting from the scheduling software to a spreadsheet. The view first filters to obtain incomplete tasks over the desired look-ahead time; often 30 to 60 days for projects of several months or more. Then sort by the impact on the project buffer with a secondary sort by task start date. This groups the tasks into chains so you can look for opportunities to recover buffer.

You can color-code the tasks indicative of their impact on the project buffer to improve visual control.

The buffer meeting should only discuss tasks in the red or yellow with the understanding that tasks in the green are potential candidates to offer resources to help on yellow or red tasks.

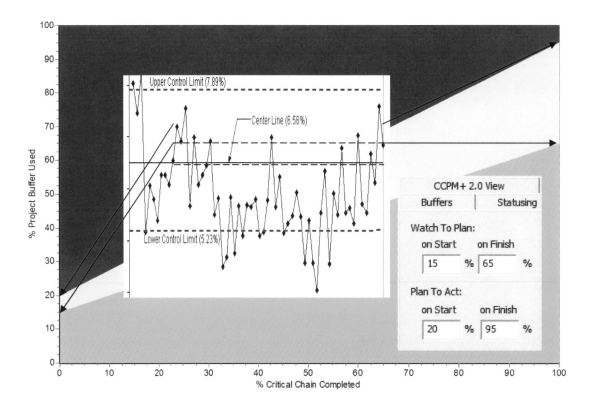

The Fever Chart Provides Visual Control for Projects. *The accompanying table directs focus on where to begin taking action.*

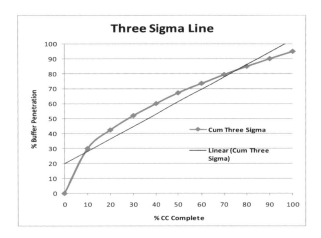

Analysis to set the initial transition lines.

Assumptions:

1. *Project comprises only the critical chain.*
2. *Ten equal tasks in the critical chain.*
3. *Task standard deviation 50% of mean.*
4. *Project buffer = 50% of critical chain.*

Purpose

The fever chart answers two questions:
1. Management's question of "When will the project complete?", and
2. The project teams' question of "When and where should we take buffer recovery action?".

The fever chart method of control seems to make logical sense and work well, but I have not been able to determine the inventor or theoretical basis.

This module suggests initial settings for your project fever charts. Once you have enough project completions (at least a dozen), you can plot your own project completion control chart, and use it to adjust the regions (See 4.3.6).

When will the project complete?

The end of the project buffer is the committed date for the project. A project which completes on or before that date succeeds on schedule. The current status of buffer penetration corresponds to the latest date estimate of project completion. You can use various tools to convert that to a projection of the finish date (See 4.4.1).

Three Regions

The fever chart identifies three color-coded regions: red, yellow, and green. The ordinate starts with zero buffer penetration, despite variation allowing projects to frequently exhibit negative buffer penetration. The fever chart plots all below zero points as zero. Some consider below zero buffer penetration as a "white" region; others as green.

The regions are often described as:
1. Green: Watch…normal variation, do nothing.
2. Yellow: Plan…for buffer recovery, but do not activate.
3. Red: Act…implement buffer recovery.

The yellow region description only applies during the earlier parts of the project (e.g. up to 50% critical chain complete), where significant recovery time exists. Later, yellow should signal taking reasonable, but not necessarily heroic, buffer recovery actions. One could also follow some control chart applications, and **use two successive points in the yellow as an action signal** (Kane, p. 68).

Critical chain software allows users to adjust the lines, as illustrated for CCPM+ on the inset.

Kane, V. (1989). Defect Prevention: Use of Simple Statistical Tools. New York: Marcel Dekker

Red Region Lower Boundary

The fever chart is a simplified control chart for the project schedule, deriving from the actual control chart for project buffer penetration at completion (see modules 4.3.6 and 9.3), illustrated by the overlay on the fever chart figure. The action threshold (yellow to red transition line) conforms to the upper control limit (or natural process limit) of the control chart for buffer penetration.

The lower graph illustrates a model for a simple project system, with assumptions shown, used to select initial end points for the red lower boundary. It plots the calculated three sigma points for the assumptions shown, and a trend line for those data points. The initial points for the red lower boundary correspond to the calculated amount on the right (95%), and the projected intersect on the left (20%).

Yellow Region Lower Boundary

Control charts are frequently divided into three regions, corresponding to one, two, or three standard deviations (illustrated for the upper half of the control chart only by the black dashed lines in the control chart overlay). Setting the green to yellow boundary on the left and right to approximately 2/3 of the red lower boundary (rounded to the nearest 5) corresponds roughly to the two-sigma line.

Predicted Results

Control charts for processes in statistical control should have 2% of the results in the top third (of the upper half of the control chart), corresponding to the yellow band of the fever chart, 14% in the middle third, and 34% in the lower third (corresponding to the green region up to ~30%) (Kane, p. 69).

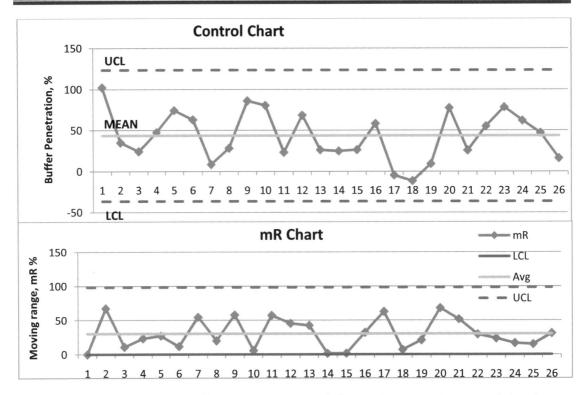

Example of Project Completion Buffer Penetration Control Charts. The appropriate control chart is called a z (zed) chart, which plots the data for single points in sequence. Control charts come in pairs: one for the range (lower), used to set the limits, and one for the value (upper), used for action.

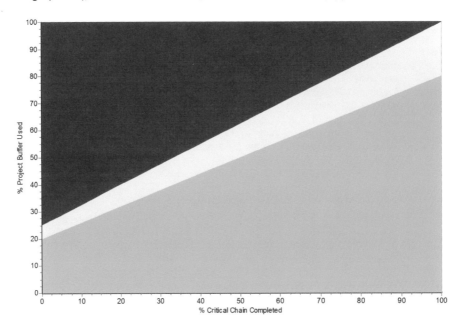

Example of Fever Chart Limits Conformed to Control Chart. *Compare to 4.3.5 chart.*

Purpose   Adjust the fever chart, task estimates, and/or buffer policy to match your project system performance and achieve projects on time, "all" the time.

Prepare Control Charts   Control charts of buffer penetration for completed projects (schedule control charts) enable you to continuously improve your project delivery system. See 9.3 for constructing control charts. The figures are an example pair of control charts. While they are reasonable examples, your charts may look quite different and suggest different actions from those displayed.

Analyze   Analyze the control charts to decide what action you need to take on your project control system, including setting new fever chart boundaries. The first steps are:

1. Determine if the process is stable; i.e. few points outside the control limits.
2. Determine if the range of variation is acceptable. It should be less than $\pm$ 100% from lower control limit (LCL) to upper control limit (UCL).

If the process is not stable, you must remove the causes of the out of control points. If the process is stable, but the variation too large, you must reduce variation: use the Six Sigma tools to do so. Start by confirming that task behavior expectations have been achieved; e.g. using buffer-based task dispatching, little or no multitasking, and no evidence of Parkinson's law. Once you have a stable process with reasonable variation, you are ready to reset the fever chart limits.

It you cannot take actions that achieve control within $\pm$ 100% of your current buffers, then you must revise your buffer sizing policy to increase the relative buffer.

Adjust Fever Chart   Most of the time your resulting moving range chart will have a non-zero mean, implying a bias in buffer penetration, as shown (Leach, 2003). The model used to set the initial fever chart lines (4.3.5) assumed only random variation. The updated model should address this difference.

Yellow/red transition:

➤ Set the right x = 100% intercept at or near 100% buffer penetration.
➤ Set the left (x=0) intercept at 20% plus about 10% of the bias; i.e. of the mean of control chart. For the example, mean = 40, implying about 25% total.

Compare the chart on the left with the one in 4.3.5. The green/yellow transition was revised to:

➤ Set the x=100% intercept corresponding to the two-sigma line on the control chart. That is, it should be at the expected mean (40% for the example) plus 2/3 of one-half the range (80% for the example) of the control chart (total 80 for example).
➤ Set the left (x=0) green/yellow transition line to be between zero and the yellow/red line in the same proportion as the right limit (20 for example).

Note that the numbers are rounded to the nearest 5%.

Leach, L. (2003). Schedule and Cost Buffer Sizing: How to account for the bias between project performance and your model. Newtown Square, PA: Project Management Institute, PM Journal, Volume 34, Number 2, pp. 34-47

Project Name _____

PM:_____

Contact Number: _____**Email:**_____

Project WEB:_____

Buffer Status Date:_____

% PB Used:_____

% CC Cpl. :_____

Buffer Status:
☐ Act
☐ Plan
☐ Watch

Actions to Unstick Tasks:

#	WBS	Task Mgr.	Due	Action

Actions to Recover Buffer:

#	WBS	Task Mgr.	Due	Action

Example Buffer Recovery Planning Form.

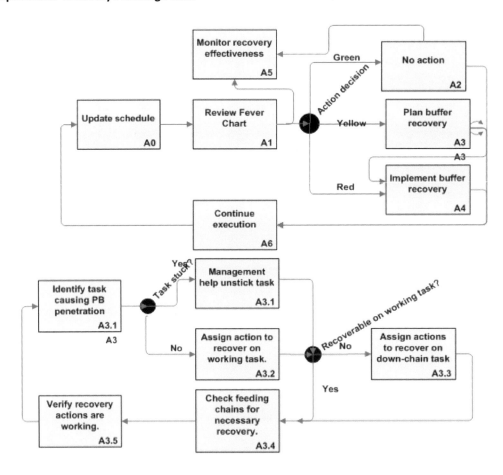

Buffer Recovery Process Flow. _PB is Project Buffer. A3 connects the lower (more detailed) chart to the upper; i.e. the lower process expands on A3 of the upper process._

Purpose
Buffer recovery acts to complete the project on or before the target date; i.e. with less than 100% buffer penetration. Buffer recovery should work to complete all projects as soon as possible.

Unstick
The first step of buffer recovery ensures that the task identified as causing the most project buffer penetration is on a path to complete as soon as possible. Ensure it is not stuck so that it can complete. This may require material or labor resources, decisions, expediting, or work-around. Since a stuck task causing maximum buffer penetration delays the value stream of the project, the cost of efforts to unstick a task are normally insignificant relative to the benefit.

Recover
Use the form to plan and track buffer recovery. If the project is in the first 50% of the critical chain, you should plan sufficient buffer recovery to bring buffer penetration back to zero before the project completes, because some of your efforts may not work. Buffer recovery planning looks for opportunities down the chain from the task causing buffer penetration. Options to recover buffer include:

1. Eliminate unnecessary tasks.
2. Parallel performance of tasks.
3. Initiate tasks before the predecessor completes, including completing a task out-of-sequence.
4. Assign most skilled resource(s).
5. Add resources:
    a. Overtime
    b. Extended work week
    c. Additional personnel
    d. Supplemental personnel to offload part of the work of the task duration driving resources
6. Change the task process.

It may not be feasible to find sufficient recovery opportunities later in the project to bring the buffer back to zero; nonetheless buffer recovery should plan to over-achieve.

Parallel Chains
Sometimes task chains parallel to the one causing the most buffer penetration are not far behind; i.e. are causing only a little less buffer impact than the most penetrating task. The Project Chain View (see 4.3.4) provides visibility into this. If it is the case, then include the parallel chains in the buffer recovery plan.

Buffer Recovery Plan
A written buffer recovery plan ensures commitment and execution. Accountability for the buffer recovery plan should rest with one person. Others can be assigned to assist. Often the task manager of the stuck task is assigned this responsibility, but if unsticking the task is a substantial effort for that person, assign buffer recovery to someone else, perhaps a resource manager.

At a recent critical chain conference, Thomas Rennert of ABB commented that "Low WIP requires a culture of fast issue resolution and fast execution". Task managers should rapidly escalate tasks needing help, and more senior management must focus on rapid response to help.

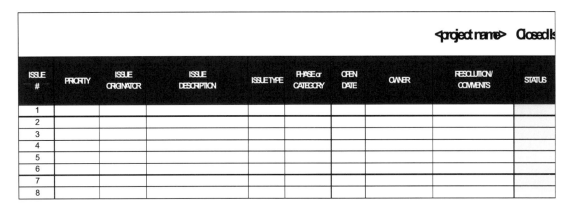

ISSUE #	PRIORITY	ISSUE ORIGINATOR	ISSUE DESCRIPTION	ISSUE TYPE	PHASE or CATEGORY	OPEN DATE	OWNER	RESOLUTION/ COMMENTS	STATUS
1									
2									
3									
4									
5									
6									
7									
8									

Example Project Issue/Action Control Log. The log should simplify identifying the queue of outstanding changes and sum the impact of submitted and approved baseline changes.

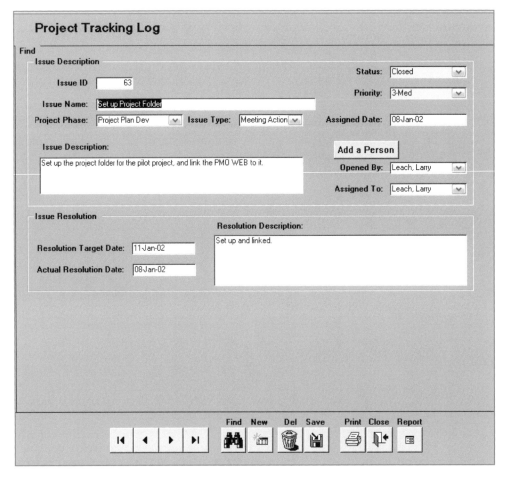

Example Issue/Action Management Database Screen

Purpose   Manage project issues and action assignments to ensure resolution and completion to support project goals.

Issues and Actions   Project issues are anything that requires a decision to enable the project to proceed. Project actions are specific tasks outside the project schedule network which must be performed to enable the project to proceed. Project actions include preparing and executing buffer management.

The information and process necessary to manage issues and actions is the same.

One person must be accountable for each issue or action. While many people may need to be involved in or consulted to make the decision or carry out the action or actions, if accountability is given to more than one person (by name!), the chances are very high that nothing will happen.

Process   The issue/action process must be simple and fast. Various tracking tools are available, some similar to those on the facing page. The essential information for an effective issue/action process was summarized by Rudyard Kipling (1902), and is sometimes captured as "Six Ws and an H":

I keep six honest serving-men,
(They taught me all I knew);
Their names are What and Why and When,
And How and Where and Who.

As long as your process ensures these, and does them fast, it should work fine.

The RACI matrix identifies four participatory responsibility types, which are then assigned to different roles in the action or issue resolution. These responsibilities types make up the acronym RACI.

- ✓ Responsible - Those who do work to achieve the task. There can be multiple resources responsible.
- ✓ Accountable - (Also Approver) The resource ultimately answerable for the correct and thorough completion of the task. There must be only one A specified for each task.
- ✓ Consulted - Those whose opinions are sought. Two-way communication.
- ✓ Informed - Those who are kept up-to-date on progress. One-way communication.

The RACI matrix may be appropriate for more monumental actions or issues, but do not let it interfere with speed and results.

Closing   Closure determines effective action and issue management. Once you are 10% into your project, if your action/issue closure rate does not significantly exceed your action/issue arrival rate, your project could be in trouble. Be sure to follow up the status of actions prior to each project meeting, and report the queue status and trend.

Change Control Log

Project #: _____
Project Name: _____

ID#	Description	Reason	Impacts		Submitted By	Submitted Date	Disposition	Disposition Date
			Budget	Schedule				
001								
002								
003								
004								
005								
006								
007								
008								
009								
010								

Example Project Change Control Log. The log should simplify the process to identify the queue of outstanding changes and sum the impact of submitted and approved baseline changes.

Procedure for Change Management

#		Procedure Step	
1	Requestor	Open the Change Form.	
2	Requestor	Fill in the header information, WBS #, Change Description, Reason for Change, and Schedule and Cost Impact, your name and date.	
3	Requestor	Submit to project change coordinator.	
4	Change Coordinator	Enter in change log and put number on change form.	
5	Change Coordinator	Send to PM	
6	Project Manager	Review and Disposition.	
7		If: Project Change	Else
	Change Coordinator	Submit to Project Owner for approval	Return to project coordinator
8	Project Owner	Disposition, and return to change coordinator.	
9	Change Coordinator	File dispositioned change, update change log and distribute.	
10	Project Scheduler	Implement approved changes in project baseline, or deviations in project working plan.	

Purpose   Control project changes to satisfy all stakeholder requirements. Avoid the common excuse of project "scope creep", which only can happen if changes are not controlled.

What is a Change?   A project change is change in the specifications for the project deliverable (scope change) or in the assumptions made in the project plan that can significantly impact project delivered scope, schedule, cost, or quality. Approved project changes authorize changing the baseline project plan, including the WBS, schedule, and budget for the project. The baseline project plan is the one the stakeholders approved in the Project Plan.
Differences between actual and estimated quantities are not project changes. Items that might cause a significant (i.e. greater than about 20% of respective buffers) change in project schedule or cost, or any other specified project goal, should be noted as deviations and communicated to all stakeholders.

Change Requests   Project delivery systems should be change friendly; i.e. plan for the inevitable need. To that end, a simple change form should encourage any project stakeholder to submit proposed changes whenever they wish. The change control process must operate at a speed appropriate to the project velocity. If your project is less than a year long, you cannot afford to have changes wait for a month or more from submission until final approval. You also cannot afford to have a large queue of pending changes, as it alone can de-motivate a project team. "Why work hard on this, it's going to change anyway…"

Change Impact   Effective change management assesses the impact of potential changes before they are approved to change the project baseline. The impact of project changes depends on when they are introduced. Generally, changes posed later in the project can have much larger impact on project performance than changes introduced early. For example, changes to concrete in the early phases of creating the design drawings may have little or even positive impact on cost and schedule. Changes made after the concrete is poured can have huge impact, including removal of what was already done. Likewise for IT projects, changes made during the initial requirements phase can have little or positive impact on the overall project goals. Changes made late in the project can require changes going back to the specifications, changes in many other modules, retesting, new documentation, etc.
Many small changes can accumulate to cause a change impact that is much larger than a simple sum of the individual changes. If many small changes are accumulating, it may be appropriate to process a "cumulative change" change request, to account for this non-linear impact.
Consequently, the change control process must estimate the impact the change would have on all project key success factors before the final decision to adopt the change. A formal change form assures this.

Change Process   The table on the facing page outlines a simple change management process that has worked on many large projects. The upper figure is an example change log. On larger projects, a change administrator owns and operates the process. The process includes a change log, containing the content illustrated in the example in the upper figure, a change control form that requires processing to estimate the change impact before decision.

Riverside Nuclear Station Unit # 5	**Supersize Project Status Report**	NSM #	12345

Project Manager: Jason Getitdone, X 4042   **Report Date:** 4/30/06

Project Scope and Business Case:
This project replaces all aging electrical equipment in the Riverside plant with new, low maintenance and enhanced operability digital controls. The replacement increases plant efficiency by 3%, and reduces ongoing maintenance cost by $3 million per year.

Project Status and Prediction Summary:
Project is 50% complete and on-track to complete within schedule and budget, and satisfy all scope requirements. Management attention needed to close issues faster than new ones arise. No insurmountable issues exist.

Schedule Trend: Cost Trend:

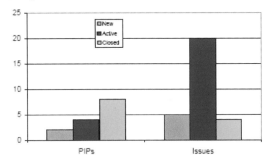

Key Milestones	End Date	Buffer %	Projected	Project Cost vs. Budget	
Design Complete	5/15/2006	10	5/1/2006	Total Authorized Budget	$25,000,000
Material Delivered	8/25/2006	50	8/15/2006	Cost Buffer (Included)	$5,000,000
Outage Pkg Delivered	12/15/2006	15	11/1/2006	Actual Cost of Work Performed	$12,530,000
Project Complete	3/15/2007	25	2/5/2007	Projected Cost At Completion	$20,750,000

Quality Trends:

Additional Project Information

Changes	Number	Sch Imp	$ Imp
Total Initiated	15	-25 days	+ $350 K
Approved	10	-25 days	+$ 125 K
Declined	2	+10 days	+ $200 K
Pending	3	0 days	+ $25K

Notes:
1. Changes approved to align work with newly identified interface requirements.
2. Contracts let for all major equipment at or below estimated amounts.

Example One-page Project Report. *Your details may vary, but this one-page report carries the information necessary for weekly or monthly reports on most projects. (PIPs are a form of defect.)*

Purpose   Project reports communicate status and trends to project stakeholders, and assist escalation of support needs when necessary.

General Content   Limit the report to one page. You should be able to summarize status on even the largest projects on one page. The report presents three content groups, roughly divided in thirds on the page. The upper third presents administrative information and a text summary of the status and projection. This is where escalation of support should be requested if needed. The administrative information includes information on the project and whom to contact, including contact information, for follow-up. The middle third presents schedule and cost information, and the lower third presents additional information as appropriate for your projects.

If possible, the report should provide access to drill down for more detail for those who need it but should not push more information on users than is necessary.

Schedule and Cost   Schedule and cost reporting uses the fever charts and tables. Note that the bottom entry on the schedule and cost tables directly answers management's most frequent questions, i.e.

- When are you going to be done?
- How much will it cost?

A convention must be established for those predictions. Prediction ranges are preferable to single point estimates.

Additional Information   The lower third of the report presents information specific to your environment or the project. The example illustrates a graph indicative of quality performance on the project; e.g. defects, bugs, or rework, and textual information on project changes.

Frequency   Report frequency depends on your project and on stakeholder's needs. Shorter projects might require daily or continuous updates; projects that are a few months long require weekly updates, and projects that are years long require monthly updates at this summary reporting level.

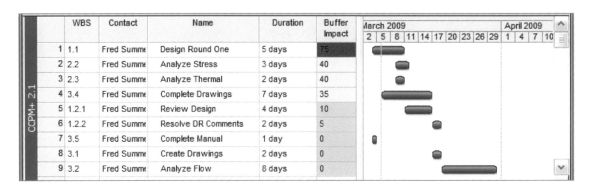

	WBS	Contact	Name	Duration	Buffer Impact	
1	1.1	Fred Summe	Design Round One	5 days	75	
2	2.2	Fred Summe	Analyze Stress	3 days	40	
3	2.3	Fred Summe	Analyze Thermal	2 days	40	
4	3.4	Fred Summe	Complete Drawings	7 days	35	
5	1.2.1	Fred Summe	Review Design	4 days	10	
6	1.2.2	Fred Summe	Resolve DR Comments	2 days	5	
7	3.5	Fred Summe	Complete Manual	1 day	0	
8	3.1	Fred Summe	Create Drawings	2 days	0	
9	3.2	Fred Summe	Analyze Flow	8 days	0	

Example Multiproject (Program or Portfolio) Task Manager Prioritized Task List. *This report prioritizes tasks for a task manager across multiple projects.*

#	Project	% Cpl	Buffer	BASELINE BCWSt	CB	BAC	CURRENT BCWS	BCWP	ACWP	EAC Min*	Max*
1	Alpha	38%	60%	$39,288	$10,000	$49,288	$21,000	$15,000	$21,000	$45,288	$55,003
2	Beta	21%	20%	$10,000	$2,500	$12,500	$2,000	$2,100	$2,600	$10,500	$12,381
3	Gamma	74%	78%	$39,340	$9,000	$48,340	$30,000	$29,000	$36,000	$46,340	$48,836
4	Delta	47%	-23%	$55,000	$13,000	$68,000	$25,000	$26,000	$23,000	$52,000	$48,654
5	Epsilon	98%	30%	$20,000	$5,000	$25,000	$19,000	$19,500	$21,000	$21,500	$21,538
6	Sigma	3%	2%	$120,000	$30,000	$150,000	$2,000	$3,000	$3,500	$120,500	$140,000
7											
8											
9											
	TOTAL	33%	36%	$283,628	$34,750	$318,378	$99,000	$94,600	$107,100	$296,128	$321,105
	CB Factor	0.5									

Table Accompanying Multiproject Cost Fever Chart Projects Project Completion. *Red Estimates at Completion (EAC) exceed the project Budget at Completion (BAC).*

#	Project	CC	Buffer	Due Date	PB (days)	Current Prediction Min*	Max*
1	Alpha	10%	15%	7/25/2007	30	6/29/2007	8/9/2007
2	Beta	85%	66%	8/15/2007	60	7/25/2007	8/1/2007
3	Gamma	50%	30%	9/15/2007	90	7/14/2007	8/10/2007
4	Delta	40%	60%	10/15/2007	30	10/3/2007	10/30/2007
5	Epsilon	25%	30%	11/15/2007	60	10/4/2007	11/27/2007
6	Sigma	5%	25%	12/15/2007	90	10/8/2007	12/9/2008
7	Donut	70%	75%	1/15/2008	90	12/23/2007	1/21/2008
8							
9							
10							

Table Accompanying Multiproject Schedule Fever Chart Predicts Project End Date. Red "Max" dates exceed the project Due Date.

Purpose

Multiproject control ensures support needs escalate to the level able to aid execution. Although most decisions are made at the project and program level, multiproject information helps resource managers and other stakeholders ensure that actions to aid one project do not adversely affect other projects. Multiproject control information often helps identify resources available to support across projects.

Multiproject Information

Multiproject information includes:
- ✓ Project pipeline (start and finish dates for all projects)
- ✓ Multiproject schedule control chart
- ✓ Multiproject schedule fever chart and projection table
- ✓ Multiproject task manager and resource prioritized task lists
- ✓ Multiproject cost control chart
- ✓ Multiproject cost fever chart and projection table
- ✓ Multiproject report
- ✓ Individual project reports
- ✓ Resource demand projections

Some organizations package information for resource managers similar to project reports for project managers.

Schedule and Cost

Schedule and cost reporting uses the multiproject fever charts and tables. Note that the bottom entry on the schedule and cost tables directly answers management's most frequent questions, i.e.
- ➢ When are you going to be done?
- ➢ How much will it cost?

The range of projections illustrated in the fever chart table (see figure) provide meaningful estimates. The lower number or date assumes no additional buffer penetration, while the upper number assumes the rate of buffer consumption continues.

The multiproject cost fever chart adds an important feature: overall program cost buffer status. As with schedule buffers, controlling the cost buffer at an aggregate level allows for more variation at the single project level; i.e. a multiproject cost buffer can be less than the sum of the individual cost buffers.

Multiproject Resource Buffer

Some organizations have introduced the idea of a multiproject resource buffer. This is a group of skilled people who are able to render assistance when projects become stuck or simply need additional resources to recover buffer. These resources are not otherwise assigned to project tasks. (Note: Eli Goldratt introduced another "resource buffer" early in critical chain history. It was a different idea which has been replaced by prioritized task lists.)

Frequency

Report frequency depends on your projects and on stakeholder's needs. Multiproject reporting intervals can usually be longer than for individual projects because the control actions usually have a longer time horizon; e.g. obtaining more resources. Multiproject reporting intervals should be at least monthly.

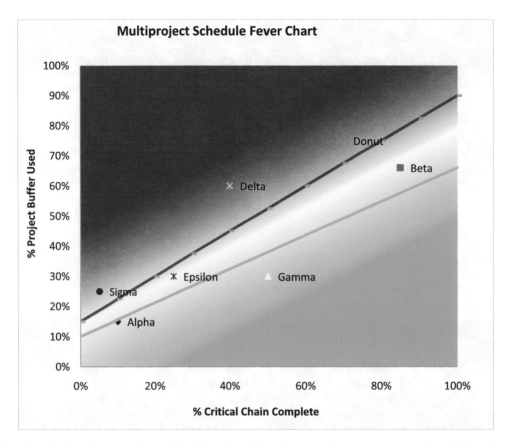

Multiproject Schedule Fever Chart. This chart identifies where senior management should focus its assistance.

#	Project	CC	Buffer	Due Date	PB (days)	Current Prediction	
						Min*	Max*
1	Alpha	10%	15%	7/25/2007	30	6/29/2007	8/9/2007
2	Beta	85%	66%	8/15/2007	60	7/25/2007	8/1/2007
3	Gamma	50%	30%	9/15/2007	90	7/14/2007	8/10/2007
4	Delta	40%	60%	10/15/2007	30	10/3/2007	10/30/2007
5	Epsilon	25%	30%	11/15/2007	60	10/4/2007	11/27/2007
6	Sigma	5%	25%	12/15/2007	90	10/8/2007	12/9/2008
7	Donut	70%	75%	1/15/2008	90	12/23/2007	1/21/2008
8							
9							
10							

Multiproject Schedule Table. The table projects the range of project schedule completion.

Purpose

Multiproject fever charts provide the primary control information for program and portfolio managers.

Multiproject Schedule Fever Chart

The multiproject schedule fever chart plots a single point for each project. It tells senior management which projects are likely to require support; i.e. those with the greatest buffer penetration.

The table accompanying the multiproject schedule fever chart provides the due date for the project (end of project buffer), and projections based on the schedule progress to date. The Excel spreadsheet turns the projections red if they exceed the due date.

.

Multiproject Cost Fever Chart

Module 2.3.2 illustrates and describes the multiproject cost fever chart.

Projections

Projections of the final end date for projects and final cost should provide an indication of variation. In both cases, two assumptions enable simple predictions of a range of final buffer use:

1. The amount of buffer use to date is the amount of buffer use that will exist at project completion; e.g. if a project has completed 50% of the critical chain and used 50% of the buffer, it will use 50% of the buffer at project completion.
2. The end of project buffer use is a linear projection of the amount of buffer use to date; e.g. if a project has completed 50% of the critical chain and used 50% of the buffer, it will use 100% of the buffer by project completion.

For cost projection, the second alternative corresponds to using the Earned Value (EV) Cost Performance Index (CPI) to project the estimate at completion. EV does not have a method to predict final schedule, although a relatively new add-on method called Earned Schedule provides a similar method.

Frequency

Multiproject charts should be prepared at the same frequency as individual project fever charts; i.e. from once per shift to no less frequent than once per week.

Integrating Schedule and Cost

The schedule and cost buffers together suggest ranges of actions.

1. Schedule Green, Cost Green: No corrective action required.
2. Schedule Green, Cost Red: Corrective action required to control cost. The corrective action can allow some amount of schedule impact.
3. Schedule Red, Cost Green: Corrective action required to control schedule. Corrective actions can increase actual cost.
4. Schedule Red, Cost Red: Corrective action required on both schedule and cost. Actions taken to reduce actual schedule should favor no or little cost action alternatives.

Generally, recovering schedule makes economic sense because it accelerates the project's benefit stream.

4.4.2 Multiproject (Program or Portfolio) Report

All Nuclear Stations	**Supersize Program Status Report**	NSM #	54321

Program Manager: Elaine Didit, X 2405   Report Date: 4/30/06

Program Scope and Business Case:
This program replaces all aging electrical equipment in all nuclear plants with new, low maintenance and enhanced operability digital controls. The replacement increases plant efficiency by 3%, and reduces ongoing maintenance cost by $3 million per plant year.

Program Status and Prediction Summary:
Projects for units 1, 2 and 5 are on target to deliver full scope at or below estimated budget and schedule. Unit 3 has exercised schedule buffer recovery to compensate for late expected hardware delivery. Unit 4 is on schedule, but has initiated cost buffer recovery to absorb higher than estimated costs on software implementation. Management has focused on PIP closure rate.

Schedule Status: Cost Status:

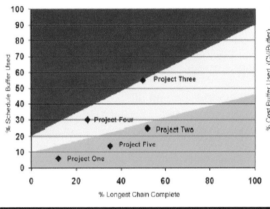
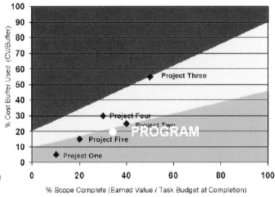

Key Milestones	End Date	Buffer %	Projected	Program Cost vs. Budget	
Project One	5/15/2006	8	5/1/2006	Total Authorized Budget	$99,000,000
Project Two	8/25/2006	22	8/15/2006	Management Reserve (Included)	$5,000,000
Project Three	12/15/2006	55	11/1/2006	Management Reserve Allocated	$1,750,000
Project Four	7/11/2006	30	6/15/2006	Actual Cost of Work Performed	$37,530,000
Project Five	3/15/2007	12	2/5/2007	Projected Cost At Completion	$95,750,000

Quality Trends:

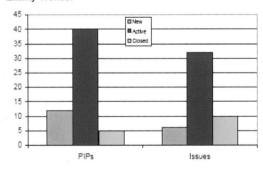

Additional Project Information

Changes	Number	Sch Imp	$ Imp
Total Initiated	30	-25 days	+ $350 K
Approved	20	-25 days	+$ 125 K
Declined	5	+10 days	+ $200 K
Pending	5	0 days	+ $25K

Notes:
1. Changes approved to align work with newly identified interface requirements.
2. Contracts let for all major equipment at or below estimated amounts.

Example One-page Multiproject (Program or Portfolio) Report. Your details may vary, but this one-page report carries the information necessary for weekly or monthly reports on most programs.

4.4.2 Multiproject (Program or Portfolio) Report

Purpose   Multiproject reports communicate status and trends to program or portfolio stakeholders on a related group of projects, and assist escalation of support needs when necessary. The report layout closely matches the single project report (4.3.10), which provides the first level of drill-down information, including contact information and schedule and cost trends by project.

General Content   Limit the report to one page or screen. You should be able to summarize status on programs or portfolios of up to approximately a dozen projects on one page. More projects than that will render the multiproject fever charts difficult to read. In those cases, you should sub-divide the projects in groups, with the top-level report showing group data instead of individual project data. The report format follows the single-project layout, which facilitates drill-down. It presents the same three content groups, roughly divided in thirds on the page. The upper third presents administrative information and a text summary of the status and projection. This is where escalation of support should be requested if needed. The administrative information includes information on the program and who to contact, including contact information for follow-up. The middle third presents schedule and cost information, and the lower third presents additional information as appropriate for your programs.
If possible, the report should provide access to drill down for more detail for those who need it, but should not push more information on users than is necessary.

Schedule and Cost   Schedule and cost reporting uses the fever charts and tables. Note that the bottom entry on the schedule and cost tables directly answers management's most frequent questions, i.e.
- When are you going to be done?
- How much will it cost?

A convention must be established for those predictions. Prediction ranges are preferable to single point estimates.
The multiproject cost fever chart adds an important feature: overall program cost buffer status. As with schedule buffers, controlling the cost buffer at an aggregate level allows for more variation at the single project level. That is, the aggregate buffer is less than the sum of the single project buffers.

Additional Information   The lower third of the report presents information specific to your environment or the program. The example illustrates a graph indicative of quality performance on the program; e.g. defects, bugs, or rework, and textual information on program changes.

Frequency   Report frequency depends on your program and on stakeholder's needs. Shorter programs might require daily or continuous updates; programs that are a few months long require weekly updates, and programs that are years long require monthly updates at this summary reporting level.

5. LPM

I learned the power of using a Project Plan to guide project execution early in my career. I learned it on a large project that did not have one for the first three years I worked on it. Despite the good intentions and hard work of several hundred people, the project without a plan continued to experience monumental issues and ever slipping schedules. When the new management team came on board, announcing they were stopping the project for six months to create this thing called a Project Plan, everyone on the project bemoaned the loss of positive work during that period, and whined about creating "paperwork" instead of good technical progress.

Management completed the Project Plan in about three months. It didn't take the full time efforts of everyone involved; most of the workers continued working on their technical tasks. Once the Project Plan was complete, we were in for another shock. We had to actually use it. We had to follow the procedures it contained. We had to status our schedules weekly, and take actions on the status. We had to use the change control processes when there were changes from the plan. We had to communicate in terms of the Work Breakdown Structure (WBS). And so on.

After a few months, we noticed that things had calmed down on the project. The issues the management team had to deal with before just did not arise any more. More interesting, we saw work progress compared to the baseline schedule at what seemed to be an astonishing rate. We were able to celebrate major accomplishments every three months. Before very long, we were able to celebrate project accomplishments that had eluded the project for years. From the point of completing the Project Plan on, the project never missed another milestone, usually completed early, and was always under budget. We became the model for success to our customer.

Many of us became staunch advocates of the Project Plan, and execution to it through effective status and measurement against schedule and cost, as the keys to project success. Complaints about the work needed to create an effective plan disappeared. Many of the members of that management team went on to become successful leaders of large projects and programs. The company became known throughout our industry as the experts in successful project execution.

Several years later the Project Management Institute was formed, and sometime after that they published the first PMBOK™ Guide. I became aware of them a few years later and was pleased to find that the PMBOK™ Guide institutionalized almost exactly the process I had learned, and by then used in a number of companies to create project success.

On the other hand, I was horrified at the size of the PMBOK™ Guide, which has now exceeded 500 pages. I had learned in the intervening years the importance of scaling Project Plans to the projects and their environment. I had also learned that leadership was more important than the paper. One needed the processes for success, but writing procedures did not mean anyone actually used them. So I put together my own LPM process, and emphasize those two things in applying it: 1) adjust it to the needs of your project or program, and 2) focus on leading the execution of whatever you decide is necessary. This section summarizes what I believe to matter most.

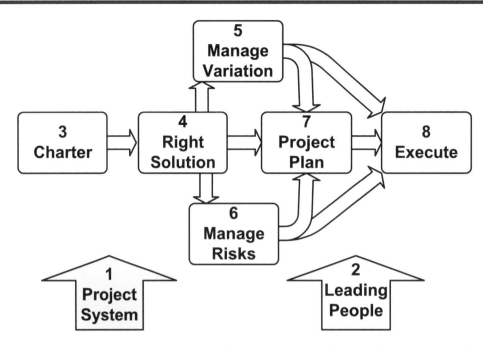

The Lean Project Management (LPM) Project Delivery System Includes Key Elements Essential to Most Projects. *Tailor the system to meet the most common needs of your projects.*

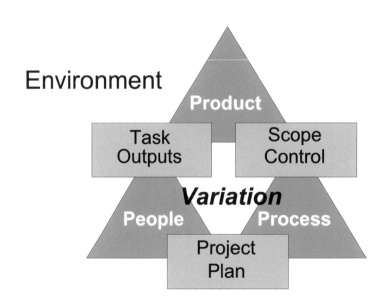

Underlying Elements Determine the System. *Exceptions will arise in all systems. A system that allows exceptions is more flexible than a system that seeks to design for all cases.*

LPM System

The LPM system for successful project delivery features eight principles. You must tailor the details of the system to the needs of your projects and project stakeholders. All systems require:

1. Leading people,
2. Project plans, and
3. Execution, including control.

LPM system design explicitly accounts for variation in inputs, processes, and outputs. Other elements of the system may have different names, e.g. chartering of projects can be any process that authorizes projects for planning, but all systems have all of the essential functions to some degree.

Leach, L. (2005). *Lean Project Management*. Booksurge.

**Product
People
Process**

Beginning with the end in mind focuses on customer satisfaction with the product: the end result of projects. People deploy processes to build the product. The relationships between the three entities are as important as the entities. For example, how people are assigned to work on tasks (the process steps of a project) affects both the speed of the process (project duration) and product quality. Consider these elements and their relationships as you operate and design changes to your system.

Environment

Each project delivery system functions within a specific project environment. For example, projects for the federal government must adhere to a large number of procurement regulations and policies of the particular agency that contracts for them, such as requiring Earned Value reporting on larger projects. Company internal projects entail other considerations. Assure that your project delivery system meets the needs of all stakeholders in your project environment.

Variation

All things vary, from the smallest imaginable world of quantum mechanics to the dynamic universe of motion and the birth and death of stars and galaxies. The LPM system builds on the reality of variation in project tasks, including the Six Sigma focus on reducing variation and theory of constraints perspective of managing variation and its impact on the flow of work through dependent steps and a constraint. LPM explicitly applies the Six Sigma thinking idea of special and common cause variation to differentiate two ways of controlling variation: project risk management for the first, and buffers for the second.

Execution

Unlike systems that emphasize the formal "paperwork" elements of project delivery (e.g. reports, plans), LPM focuses on execution. The system develops and delivers the flow of work to satisfy customer needs. It starts from viewing the system from the perspective of those that have to do the work, and the relationships between them that cause the work to flow.

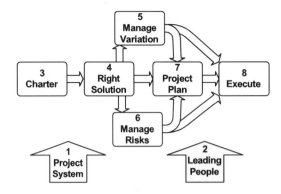

Leading People Drives Project Success. *Leadership, rather than management, matters most.*

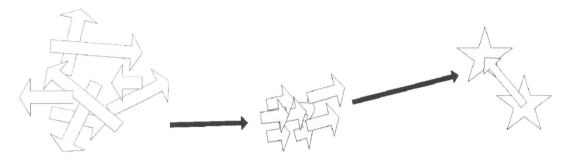

Leaders Forge a Team from Diverse Individuals. *The star represents the goal, which may move during project execution.*

#	Item	Project Client	Project Leader	Project Scheduler	Project Administrator	Work Package Manager	Resource Manager	Task Manager	Resource	Senior Management	Contractors
						Stakeholder					
1	Project Charter	A	R	I	I	I	I	I	I	I	
2	Project Plan	A	R	I	I	I	I	I	I	I	
3	Project Processes		A	I	R	I	C	I	I	I	I
4	Project Requirements	A,R	C	I		C	C	I			I
5	Project Scope Statement		A	R		C	C				I
6	Project Change Log		A	C	R	I	I	I	I	I	I
7	Project Risk Registry		A	C		C	C	C		I	I
8	Project Schedule		A	R	I	C	C	I	I	I	I
9	Project Budget	A	R	I	I	C	C			I	I

RACI Matrix Applied to Project Stakeholders Relative to Project Team Deliverables. *A similar matrix, organized to the WBS, applies for project deliverables.*

Leading People

I have often wondered why they don't call it project leadership instead of project management. I actively wonder why we don't use leadership instead of management whenever people are involved, because leadership is what matters with people. People determine project success. Thus, leadership matters most.

Heart and Head

Bennis provides a great list comparing leadership and management. The bottom line is that leadership concerns people, and management controls things. Projects require both leadership and management.

Abrashoff demonstrates that true leadership can exist within the confines of tightly regulated organizations. Leadership is nothing new. This verse, thousands of years old, applies:

The best leaders are those the people hardly know exist.
The next best is a leader who is loved and praised.
Next comes one who is feared.
The worst one is the leader that is despised.
If you don't trust the people,
They will become untrustworthy.
The best leaders value their words, and use them sparingly.
When she has accomplished her task, the people say,
"Amazing: we did it, all by ourselves!"
Tao Te Ching, verse 17

Bennis, W. (1989). Why Leaders Can't Lead: The Unconscious Conspiracy Continues. San Francisco: Jossey-Bass
Abrashoff, M. (2008) It's Our Ship. New York: Business Plus

Situational Leadership

Situational leadership means adjusting your leadership style to the needs of the project stakeholders in regard to their specific role on the project at hand. Even if someone was the world expert on the tasks they performed on the last project, thus capable of independent work, if on this project you have them in a new role with new performance requirements, your leadership style may need to start out more directive.
Hersey, P., Blanchard, K. and Johnson, D. (1996). Management of Organization Behavior, New Jersey: Prentice Hall

Stakeholders

Stakeholders include anyone who has an interest in or influence on a project. Stakeholders always include at least the project sponsor, project manager, project team, suppliers, and users. Stakeholders may include investors, neighbors, regulators, and other groups. Leaders address the needs of all stakeholders.

Responsibility Assignment

Project leadership demands clear responsibility assignment to all project stakeholders. The Responsibility Assignment Matrix (RAM) is the project management tool for assigning responsibility to create the project deliverables. It assigns responsibility to elements of the Work Breakdown Structure (WBS). You may extend the matrix to key stakeholders using the RACI model:
      R = Responsible (Make it happen: do it!)
      A = Accountable (Cause it to happen: delegate and follow-up.)
      C = Consulted (Approve before it happens)
      I = Inform (Need to know what happened)
Effective responsibility assignment demands follow-up and positive reinforcement.

Communicate

The leader implements through three-way communication: up, across, and down. For very small projects, intuitive communication may suffice. Large projects demand a communication plan, and the largest projects or programs may involve communication work packages and teams. See the communication plan addressed in module 7.5: it applies to any type of project.

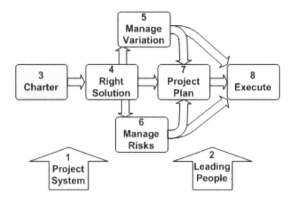

Project Chartering Starts The Project Process. *A simple rule: no charter, no project.*

Project Charter	
Project Name:	
Date:	
Project Vision (End State):	**Business Case:**
	Customer:
Purpose (Why?):	*Process:*
	Employee:
Assumptions and Constraints:	
1.	*Financial:*
2.	*Estimated Return: $ $/year*
3.	*Duration of Returns: years*
4.	*Estimated Project Cost:*
	ROI: 64 + 16
Project Organization Linkage:	*Team and Individual Responsibility:*
Measures of Success:	**Operating Guidelines:**
Approvals:	
	Project Leader
	Client/Sponsor

Example Charter Form.

Project Charter

The Project Management Institute (PMI, p. 81) defines the project charter as, "**A document issued by the project initiator or sponsor that authorizes the existence of a project and provides the project manager with the authority to apply organizational resources to project activities.**"

The project charter can serve multiple purposes from proposing projects for consideration through authorizing project execution. The name the organization uses for the charter and its use vary by organization and project type. The model I prefer for internal projects deploys the project charter in two steps; first as a decision tool to decide if a project is worthy of investing planning resources and second to authorize detailed project planning. I like to reserve actual project authorization until after completion of the detailed project plan. Projects performed under contract follow a different protocol, usually starting with a "bid/no bid" analysis, and ending with a contract; sometimes containing a detailed project plan.

PMI. (2004). A Guide to the Project Management Body of Knowledge. Third Edition.

Content

Certain elements of a project charter are universal, including:
- ➢ Authorization for the project manager
- ➢ Reasons for undertaking the project
- ➢ Objectives of the project
- ➢ Assumptions and constraints
- ➢ Identities of the main stakeholders

Additional content may be necessary specific to your situation, or to the particular project.

Why?

The business case for the project describes why the project is taking place. "Business case" applies broadly to any type of organization or project. Note the suggestion on the form to consider at least four elements of the business case: the customer, business process, employees, and financial. Add elements appropriate to your project environment.

Measures of Success

The measures of success for the project provide clear guidance to the team for how all stakeholders will judge project success. These measures should focus on the project result measures, but may include the conventional measures of project execution itself (i.e. cost, schedule, scope, and quality performance.)

Operating Guidelines

Operating guidelines in a project charter describe how the team executing to the charter should act. They may address communication guidelines, budget authority, change or quality management, or anything else important to the team executing to the charter. With the definition I propose above, these are for the planning phase of the project, not the execution phase. The execution phase operating guidelines are in the project plan.

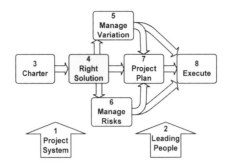

Find the Right Solution. People often seize on the first solution presented: often it is not very good

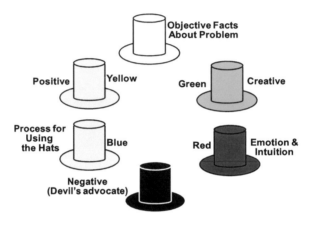

de Bono's Six Thinking Hats Enables Rapid Creative Solution Finding. *Lead your team to collectively wear one hat a time; usually starting with the blue hat to plan and summarize the process.*

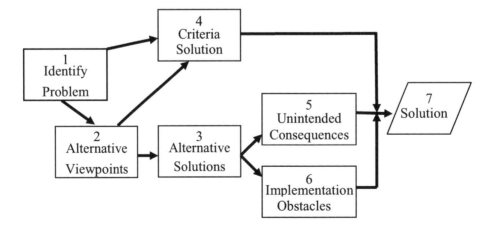

An Enhanced Process to Ensure Improved Solutions. *Developing and assessing at least three alternatives, including "do nothing", can lead to huge project improvement at little cost.*

Overall

There is no value in doing the wrong project better. Project selection and solution finding are the most important steps of any project. Too often, project teams are given a solution to implement, rather than chartered to make good on an opportunity or solve a problem. Even then, creative thinking provides insight to enable improving the solution chosen. For project portfolio selection from a TOC view, see:

Leach, L. *Applying the Theory of Constraints to Project Portfolio Management*. In Levine, H. (2003). Project Portfolio Management. New York. Jossey-Bass.

Too many project teams seize on the first solution that comes to mind. That solution frequently can be greatly improved with a small amount of thinking. You owe it to your project stakeholders to consider a range of solutions; at least three, and carefully select the best one before you proceed.

de Bono

Edward de Bono leads the world in teaching creative thinking. Best known for his **Lateral Thinking** and **Six Hats** processes, he developed and deployed many simple tools to aid creative solution-finding from the perspective of design.

de Bono. E. (1970) *Lateral Thinking*. New York: Harper & Row
de Bono. E. (1985). *Six Thinking Hats*. Boston: Little, Brown and Company

Juran

Dr. Joseph Juran is one of the U.S. "quality Gurus" who went to Japan following WW II to teach them modern quality methods. Although Juran is less well known than W. Edwards Deming, his contemporary, his methods are equally powerful. His approach focuses on the technical processes to produce quality. The following reference, one of three in a series, is an excellent place to start.

Juran, J. (1988). *Juran on Planning for Quality*. New York: The Free Press.

Heavy Artillery

Keeping in mind the TOC perspective of inherent simplicity, sometimes huge opportunities or difficult problems require more systematic approaches to creativity. The approaches described in the following two references can be scaled to any problem or opportunity, but are particularly useful for the larger opportunities.

Nadler, G. and Hibino, S. (1994) *Breakthrough Thinking*. Rocklin, CA: Prima Publicizing
Altshuller, G. (1997). 40 Principles: **TRIZ** Keys to Technical Innovation. Worcester, MA: Technical Innovation Center.

Project Implementation

Implementing the right solution through the project starts with specifying the assumptions that will guide planning and execution of the process, and using the Work Breakdown Structure (WBS) to identify all of the project deliverables and responsibility for them. Sometimes the feasibility study to select the right solution is part of the project. In that case, the project plan may need a "rolling wave" approach to plan using an initial assumed solution, with a task to plan further details once the right solution is selected.

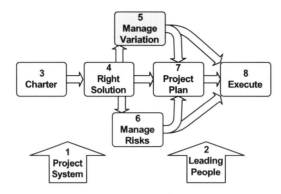

LPM/CCPM Manages Common-Cause Variation with Buffers.

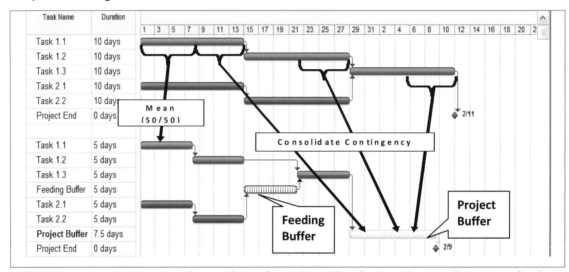

Buffers Aggregate the Variation Along a Chain of Activities. *This shortens the overall duration of a chain of tasks, and tends towards a normal distribution for the sum.*

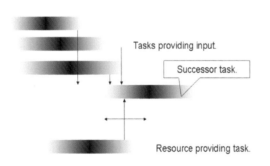

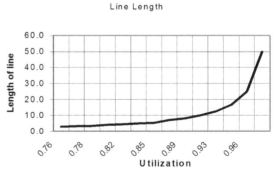

Merging of several predecessor tasks increases the likelihood of delay of the successor task. *Delay can also come from resource unavailability (queuing).*

Queuing Is Non-linear. *Resource planning must allow protective capacity.*

Variation

See 3.4.2 for a description of the fundamentals of applying profound knowledge of variation to projects. This module deals with using buffers to manage common-cause variation.

Accuracy

When it comes to comparing actual to estimate (schedule, cost), many people misapply the term accuracy. If the actual happens to match or come close to the estimate, they assert that the prediction was accurate. That is not what accuracy means. Accuracy measures the variation in the outcome of a process. It is a measure of the common-cause variation in the process. Accuracy must be expressed as plus or minus some amount; sometimes a percentage. For example, you may shoot a gun at a target (the process) 50 times, and then measure the dispersion of the holes in the target as $\pm$ 3 inches. You may then use a different gun or gun rest, or move closer to the target (change the process), and measure that the dispersion is $\pm$ 2 inches, an improvement in accuracy.

The common-cause variation in the time to perform many project tasks is usually a substantial percentage of the mean; perhaps the two-sigma range is on the order of -50% to +100%. For most project tasks, the distribution is not likely to be symmetrical. Because of this variation, it is futile to seek to predict dates for individual tasks.

Buffers

As described in 3.2.1, nature helps manage variation for chains of tasks. When you take samples and add them together to form a sum, the variation of the sum is the square root of the sum of the squares of the variation of each sample lot; i.e.:

u_i = variation of each sample lot (i.e. task)

Variation Buffer = $\sqrt{\sum u_i^2}$

Removing the variation allowance from each task, and summing it at the end of chains, allows for much less total buffering to have the same degree of schedule protection.
Better yet, even though each task may come from a process with a different and non-symmetrical completion distribution, the sum will tend towards a symmetrical normal distribution if there are more than a few tasks. The form of the normal distribution greatly improves the probability of completing within a given variation.

Queuing

Queuing theory describes the buildup of lines when there is variation in the arrival of line members and the time to process each one. Queuing is non-intuitive. Most people think that if the arrival rate and processing rate averages are equal, there will not be a line, or at most the line will be one unit (in this case, a task waiting for a resource). The line tends to grow infinitely long as the arrival rate approaches the processing rate, as illustrated by the figure.

Merging

When several predecessor tasks feed one successor task, the latest task determines the start of the successor. This moves the mean of the distribution for the start of the successor task to the right…a delay. Critical chain accounts for this for chains that feed into critical chain tasks with a feeding buffer…an allowance to reduce introducing delays to critical chain tasks from feeding chain tasks.
Critical chain tasks might also demand a resource from a non-critical chain task. Feeding buffers do not account for this. With multiple projects, the capacity constraint buffer helps by adding protective capacity for the system.

Project Buffer

If your projects have many parallel chains, you may require larger project buffers to account for merging and queuing delays.

Manage Risks With Project Management Tools. *Leadership, rather than management, matters most.*

Type	Examples	Management Method
Variation **Common-cause**	All causes of variation within the output of products/processes in statistical control (most conventional project tasks).	Projects - Buffers and action thresholds (e.g. control charts). Products – tolerances and statistical process control.
Design Uncertainty	Lack of knowledge, assumptions, difference in opinion and viewpoint.	Progressive Elaboration Robust decision making. Project or product change management.
Environmental and Internal Uncertainty	Natural events, new regulations, external-driven changes in project requirements, accidents. Failures or changes with the product or process.	**Project risk management**: (Identify, Quantify, Monitor, Prevent and Mitigate).

Different Management Methods Apply to Different Types of Uncertainty. *Conventional project risk management confounds the first and last types of variation when addressing PERT or Monte-Carlo in the sense of risk management.*

#	Risk Event	P	C	R	Trigger to Monitor	Prevention Actions	Mitigation Actions
1	As a result of a **work pressure** *management resistance to change* may result, which would lead to **delaying the benefits of LPM**.	3	3	9	Low management attendance at training. Lack of management leadership and/or tool implementation.	Management buy-in sessions. Senior management goal setting and follow through. Assurance of management availability and skill to use tools.	Support to management that is not leading the implementation. Remedial counseling by senior management.

Risk Register Guides Risk Actions. *Actions can range from assuming the risk occurs as a baseline assumption through specific actions to prevent the risk from happening (reduce probability) and/or to prepare to mitigate the effects of the risk should it occur.*

Risk Management	Risk Management seeks to control unplanned events that may affect the project results.

| **Risk Management Process** | The overall risk management process contains six steps:
1. Risk Management Planning
2. Risk Identification
3. Qualitative Risk Analysis
4. Quantitative Risk Analysis
5. Risk Response Planning
6. Risk Monitoring and Control
The last step occurs throughout project execution.
Most projects do fine with a simple risk management plan comprising an initial risk assessment, decisions on risk mitigation, and ongoing monitoring and implementation of mitigation measures.
Items with greater than a 50% chance of happening over the life of the project should be considered as baseline assumptions for the project; i.e. assume they will happen. You could then include in the risk matrix the consequences of what might happen if it does not occur. |

| **Risk Identification** | Risk identification seeks to uncover the unplanned events that might affect your project. It helps to identify risks with the script illustrated in the risk register, changing the bold wording to describe the cause and effect of each potential risk. Use the knowledge and experience of the project team to come up with an initial list of potential risks, and then hone it to the top dozen or so risks that are worth controlling through quantification, elimination by addressing it in the project plan, or combining risks into categories.
You can only control those risks that you are able to identify. You cannot identify the "unknown unknowns" that may affect your project. Thus, risk identification and management must continue throughout project execution. |

| **Risk Register** | A risk register enables risk management over the life of the project. You can begin with a table like that shown. You may choose to assign each risk to a single person to manage. The risk matrix is the main tool for response planning, monitoring, and control. |

| **Quantification** | Quantify risks as to probability and consequence using an appropriate scale. I use a three-point scale because I do not feel our ability to quantify justifies more precision. Multiply probability times consequence to get the relative risk (**R = P*C**): |

P (Probability)	C (Consequence)
3 = 21-50%	**3 = > Project (Time or Cost) Buffer**
2 = 5-20%	**2 = > 20% of Project Buffer, < Project Buffer**
1 = < 5%	**1 = < 20% of Project Buffer**

Some suggest adding a variable for the ability to control (K) the risk. They rank it on the same scale, and divide by K in the risk equation.

5.7 Project Plan

The Project Plan Immediately Precedes Execution. *A Project Plan is much more than a schedule.*

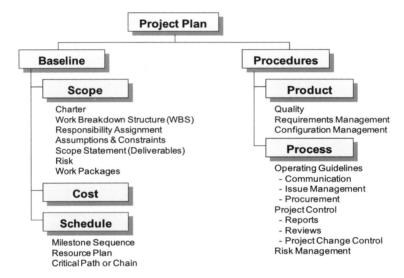

The Project Plan Contains or Refers to Everything Necessary to Guide Project Execution.

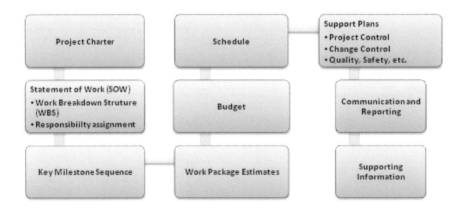

Example Process to Develop a Project Plan. *The Work Breakdown Structure (WBS) serves to assign responsibility and integrate the project.*

Project Plan

PMI defines the Project Plan, sometimes called the Project Execution Plan (PEP) or Project Management Plan (PMP), as "**A formal, approved document that defines how the project is executed, monitored, and controlled. It may be summary or detailed and may be composed of one or more subsidiary management plans and other planning documents**". In short, it contains everything anyone needs to know to execute the project. While past Project Plans usually were documents, now they often are Intranet manifestations; e.g. databases, SharePoint sites, WIKIs, or shared folders. People often mistakenly refer to a project schedule as the "project plan". A project plan is much more than a schedule, usually consisting of the elements indicated in the top figure. Scale the contents of your project plans to the size and complexity of the project. Small, simple projects may get by with a charter, budget, and schedule. Large or complex projects require a full project plan. Project plans must remain active for the life of the project.

Product

The Project Plan specifies all of the requirements for the project results. This may require a formal Statement of Work (SOW), and a formal quality plan, but always requires at least a Work Breakdown Structure (WBS) to organize the project deliverables and assign responsibility for planning and executing their creation.

Processes

The Project Plan also specifies all of the work processes necessary to plan and execute the project. Work processes should focus on the needs of the project execution team and the project stakeholders. All projects must specify the processes for:
- ➢ Quality Assurance
- ➢ Formal project change control.

Most projects should also have at least a simple matrix approach to project risk mitigation (see 5.6). Other elements of the project plan might include:
- ➢ Safety
- ➢ Security
- ➢ Privacy
- ➢ Reliability
- ➢ Maintainability

Manage Changes

All but the smallest and simplest projects experience changes during execution. Unmanaged project changes cause stakeholder dissatisfaction. While some (less than professional) project stakeholders may initially bristle at the need to formally approve seemingly small changes in project scope, budget, or schedule, many project failures attribute to a failure to manage changes. Small changes, particularly those that happen later in project execution, often accumulate to create massive impacts.

Project Kickoff

Approval of the Project Plan authorizes the project for execution. You should always start projects with a formal project execution event. All project stakeholders should attend the project kickoff to affirm their role in the project and their commitment to project success.

6. Roles

Focus is the first and most important of the three new rules. Everyone must understand and practice their roles to enhance focus. You can make substantial progress by just implementing some key management behavior changes, without getting to critical chain schedules, etc.

Mike Boissau is one of the most successful project and organizational leaders I know. Mike was the project manager for a $126 million maintenance and repair project on the nuclear aircraft carrier Eisenhower. He attended a four hour presentation on the principles of CCPM, and concluded that he wanted to try it. He couldn't change the CPM schedules that were already in place for the project, but he could affect how people behaved. He changed the job descriptions for the first level supervisors. Prior to his change, their job comprised mostly sitting in offices making sure all of their workers had valid numbers to charge to. Despite this, Mike knew that similar projects in the past over-ran both budget and schedule and that over 30% of the work was completed without charges made to it!

He told the supervisors, "I'll take care of the cost. Your job is to supervise your workers. I want you on the ship. If anything gets stuck, I want you to resolve the cause, and have the people stay on that task until it is done!" He did a few other team building things, but that was the main and hardest behavior change he focused on.

The project finished early. The project team saved $26 million. They had less than one half of the quality defects reported during inspection and sea trials, compared to previous projects. The project did not have a critical chain schedule. It was not pipelined. Supervisors (Task Managers) used their knowledge to prioritize tasks. The huge results show the power of focus.

The introduction to section 1 described the early evolution of critical chain as a scheduling technique. While these scheduling elements remain essential parts of CCPM and therefore LPM, most implementers have moved to a behavior first approach. This approach recognizes the substantial gains achievable by enabling resources to focus on one task at a time. They realize they can increase the Throughput of projects by management controlling Work in Progress (WIP) and handling tasks that need management support to keep projects flowing. The organization makes quick gains this way, while developing the individual schedules, pipelining, and learning buffer management.

This section describes a typical set of roles for successful LPM implementation in terms of their functions or behavior. You may choose to name and combine the roles differently but your process will need to account for all of the roles described. Your management team should rewrite the role descriptions specifically for your organization.

I chose to introduce and utilize the Daniels' approach to defining behavior feedback measurements for most of the roles. I believe it can be quite powerful, but understand that many organizations will be uncomfortable with the unusual degree of management rigor implied. You can use the information presented in the graphics, even if you do not choose to use the measures quantitatively for feedback.

Various Roles Support Lean Project Delivery. *You may use different names for the roles, but all functions are necessary.*

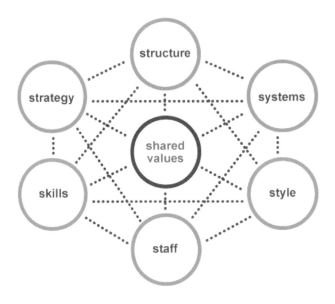

The Seven S Organizational Models Helps Relate Roles. *Peters, T. and Waterman, H. (1980). In Search of Excellence. United States: Harper and Row*

Roles

The LPM system requires functions performed by people in various roles. The first diagram illustrates the relationships of the roles; with the notion that management's role is to enable the resources to do the work. One or more people must perform each role. The Seven S organizational model helps relate the roles. Senior management has overall responsibility for the system and normally focuses on system strategy and design, including structure and staff. Mid-level managers focus more on the operational elements, such as skills, all linked by a shared system goal and values.

Functions

Effective project delivery requires design, implementation, operation, and ongoing improvement of the project system. The overall project delivery system takes project needs and inputs to deliver project results as the output. Project system roles share overlapping responsibility for the following key project functions:

> Project delivery system design.
> Portfolio Selection.
> Project Plans.
> System provisioning.
> Execution, including measurement and control.
> Project Closeout.
> Project delivery system improvement.

Collectively, management must also perform all of the functions included in the Seven S model, including developing and deploying strategy, organizing, and staffing the organization with all necessary skills to execute, including all of the Human Resource functions.

Management Roles

Management roles include senior management, resource managers, and task managers. Managers perform all of the functions above, with the % effort to each role determined by their particular role. While most managers are comfortable with the operational function, many are less skilled and therefore less comfortable with the other functions. Senior managers are mostly concerned with the design, implementation, and improvement of the system.

First and second level managers focus on helping the performing resources. They concern themselves more with operation of the system, including prompt decision making, helping resources with stuck tasks, and executing buffer recovery. All management contributes to help resources on stuck tasks and to recover buffer when necessary during execution. They promptly escalate calls for help to senior management when necessary for project flow.

Performer Roles

Performer roles include the Master Scheduler and the performing resource. The Master Scheduler performs the same functions for all project systems. The work of performing resources includes the full extremes of human endeavor. Key functions include working on and statusing their work on the task. The primary execution rule is **relay racer task performance**: focus on one task at a time fully until it is complete and pass on the result when complete. Task performers must also originate a call for help when needed to flow the work.

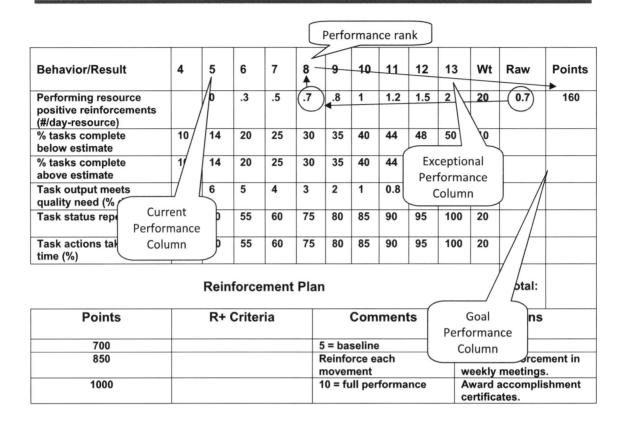

Behavior/Result	4	5	6	7	8	9	10	11	12	13	Wt	Raw	Points
Performing resource positive reinforcements (#/day-resource)		0	.3	.5	.7	.8	1	1.2	1.5	2	20	0.7	160
% tasks complete below estimate	10	14	20	25	30	35	40	44	48	50	0		
% tasks complete above estimate	1	14	20	25	30	35	40	44					
Task output meets quality need (%		6	5	4	3	2	1	0.8					
Task status rep		0	55	60	75	80	85	90	95	100	20		
Task actions ta... time (%)		0	55	60	75	80	85	90	95	100	20		

Performance rank

Current Performance Column

Exceptional Performance Column

Goal Performance Column

Reinforcement Plan

Total:

Points	R+ Criteria	Comments	...ns
700		5 = baseline	
850		Reinforce each movement	...rcement in weekly meetings.
1000		10 = full performance	Award accomplishment certificates.

Example Task Manager Performance Management Matrix. *Note that a score of 10 for all measures equals full performance, and higher scores represents outstanding.*

Results	Behaviors	Reinforcements
Tasks complete *Task output quality*	✓ Resources work on one task at a time. ✓ Perform actions necessary to ensure task output quality. ✓ Complete one task before starting another. ✓ Request help immediately if task delayed. ✓ Report task status.	✓ Verbal positive feedback on desired behaviors. ✓ Written "thank you" upon task completion. ✓ Verbal appreciation for task results quality.

Example Task Performers Effectiveness Measures.

Performance Matrix

The Performance Matrix is a tool to clarify and measure expected results and the behaviors necessary to produce the results demanded by the project delivery system. Although you need not use this powerful tool to implement LPM, you will find the actions it drives useful to make norms of the new behaviors. The following modules use it to describe the various roles of LPM.

Daniels, A. and Daniels, J. (2006). *Performance Management.* Atlanta, GA: Performance Management Pubilcations, p. 150

Matrix Considerations

The performance matrix identifies the key results and behaviors related to about 80% of the performers work: that which matters most. Set full performance at a score of 10, and current performance at a scale value of 5, because experience shows that people like a scale that allows for superior performance.

Develop Matrix

Start with a simple listing of the results, behaviors likely to cause those results, and potential reinforcements, as illustrated on the lower table on the facing page. Then create the performance matrix:
1. List the behavior/result, and the units for measuring it.
2. Determine current performance...the '5' on each column.
3. Set a goal for each Behavior/Result...the '10' on each column.
4. Assign intermediate values for intermediate performance, and greater values for exceptional performance.
5. Assign a weight rating to each Behavior/Result (total should equal 100).

Assess Performance

Keep track of the variables necessary to use the matrix. You should track the data continuously, and evaluate at least weekly. To evaluate:
1. List the actual data into the 'Raw' column.
2. Circle the value to the left that corresponds most closely to the raw data.
3. Read the performance rank off the head of the column for the circled number, and
4. Multiply that number by the weight (Wt) to calculate the Points.
5. Sum the points column to attain the total.

Reinforce

As a performer, you should review your results and consider how to improve. As a supervisor, you should reinforce the desired behaviors on a daily basis. Supervisors should review the results with the employee at least weekly, and provide appropriate reinforcement for any improvement. Many zero to very low cost reinforcements are possible. Check the references above and below. Above all, be sure to reinforce yourself!

Nelson, R. (2005). *1001 Ways to Reward Employees.* New York: Workman Publishing

Task Process Improvement

Track and trend actual task performance data for future planning and execution. Spreadsheets provide handy means to record, track, and trend your information. You should adjust the measures and goals over time as you improve your skills and work processes.

Behavior/Result	4	5	6	7	8	9	10	11	12	13	Wt	Raw	Points
Performing resource positive reinforcements (#/day-resource)		0	.3	.5	.7	.8	1	1.2	1.5	2	20		
% tasks complete below estimate	10	14	20	25	30	35	40	44	48	50	10		
% tasks complete above estimate	10	14	20	25	30	35	40	44	48	50	10		
Task output meets quality need (% defects)	7	6	5	4	3	2	1	0.8	0.5	0	20		
Task status reported (%)	50	67	75	80	85	90	95			100	20		
Task actions taken on time (%)	50	67	75	80	85	90	95			100	20		

Reinforcement Plan | Total:

Points	R+ Criteria	Comments	Plans
700		5 = baseline	
850		Reinforce each movement	Verbal reinforcement in stand-up meetings.
1000		10 = full performance	Award accomplishment certificates.

Example Task Manager Performance Management Matrix: You Must Create Your Own! *Task managers track their actual performance weekly for their own use, and review monthly with their resource manager. Note that a score of 10 for all measures equals full performance, and higher scores represents outstanding. Daniels, A. and Daniels, J. (2006). Performance Management. Atlanta, GA: Performance Management Publications, p. 150*

Results	Behaviors	Reinforcements
Tasks complete *Task output quality*	✓ Resources work on one task at a time ✓ Perform actions necessary to ensure task output quality ✓ Complete one task before starting another ✓ Request help immediately if task delayed ✓ Report task status	✓ Verbal positive feedback on desired behaviors ✓ Written "thank you" upon task completion ✓ Verbal appreciation for task results quality

Example Task Manager Effectiveness Measure: Task Performer's Results, Behaviors, and General Reinforcements.

Task Manager

The Task Manager is responsible and accountable for task completion. The Task Manager most often directly supervises the task performing resource, although sometimes he/she may be the performing resource. The most important task manager behavior is to **positively reinforce desired behaviors by task performing resources**. Task Managers can manage more than one task at a time, frequently both planning for future tasks and leading execution on present tasks.

Functions

Task Managers are responsible for the following key project functions:
➤ Task Planning
  o Identify all of the tasks necessary to complete the project deliverables.
  o Identify the relationships between the tasks.
  o Estimate the duration for the tasks.
  o Identify the resources necessary to perform the tasks.
➤ Task Execution
  o Authorize the resources to start work on a task.
  o Report task status upon start, completion, and at identified intervals.
  o Help resources get what they need to not delay tasks.
  o Escalate tasks for help when unsticking tasks requires action not within the direct control of the Task Manager.
  o Support buffer recovery.

Due to their vital role, Task Managers must be accessible at all times, or designate an alternate. Task Managers most often are first level supervisors.

Estimating Tasks

Estimate tasks to effectively apply resources to complete all of the projects in the portfolio as quickly as possible. The duration estimate should provide a 50% chance of completing the task within the duration estimate, assuming the performing resource that determines the task duration works in increments of 100% of their time. For the first critical chain project, determine this estimate by decreasing the duration estimate previously used, keeping the work the same (i.e. person-hours), to achieve at least 100% resource loading on the task, and then cut that duration in half.

Executing Tasks

Task Managers assign specific resources to perform tasks and then focus on helping the task performers complete the tasks as soon as possible. Many task managers have daily stand-up 5-10 minute meetings with their task performers to status and assign new tasks and provide direct help or escalation for help on tasks that are stuck.

Statusing Tasks

Task Managers report task status to the project manager. They provide the actual start date when tasks start, the actual finish date when tasks finish, and an estimate of remaining duration for in-progress tasks at the standardized status frequency, most often once per week on a particular day.

Task Process Improvement

Task managers should accumulate actual task performance data for future planning and execution, including a control chart of the ratio of actual task performance duration to estimated duration.

Behavior/Result	4	5	6	7	8	9	10	11	12	13	Wt	Raw	Points
Supervisor behavior reinforced (times/day)	1	2	3	5	6	8	10	12	16	20	20		
% escalated tasks cleared in one day	50	67	75	80	85	90	95	97	98	100	20		
Task output meets quality need (% defects)	7	6	5	4	3	2	1	0.8	0.5	0	20		
Multitasking: # of started but incomplete tasks per resource	4	3	2.5	2	1.8	1.6	1.5	1.4	1.2	1	20		
# tasks per 10 resources per week stopped without completing	2.5	2	1.5	1	.75	.6	.5	.4	.3	0	20		

Reinforcement Plan				Total:

Points	R+ Criteria	Comments	Plans
700		5 = baseline	
850		Reinforce each movement	Verbal reinforcement in stand-up meetings.
1000		10 = full performance	Award accomplishment certificates.

Example Resource Manager Performance Management Matrix: You Must Create Your Own! *Resource Managers track their actual performance weekly for their own use, and review monthly with their manager. Note that a score of 10 for all measures equals full performance, and higher scores represents outstanding. Daniels, A. and Daniels, J. (2006). Performance Management. Atlanta, GA: Performance Management Publications, p. 150*

Results	Behaviors	Reinforcements
Effective behaviors reinforced *Task help provided when needed* *Resources skilled in task needs* *Resources available* *Task output quality*	✓ Reinforce relay racer task behavior ✓ Dispatch one task at a time to resources ✓ Help on stuck tasks ✓ Help on buffer recovery ✓ Perform actions necessary to ensure task output quality	✓ Verbal positive feedback on desired behaviors ✓ Written "thank you" upon task completion ✓ Verbal appreciation for task results quality

Example Resource Manager Effectiveness Measure: Supervisor's Results, Behaviors, and General Reinforcements.

6.3 Resource Manager Role

Resource Manager

Resource Managers provide the resources necessary to deliver quality work on project tasks. The most important resource manager behavior is to **positively reinforce desired behaviors by supervisors**.

Functions

Resource Managers are responsible for the following key project functions:
- Support of Portfolio and Project Planning:
  - Identify all of the available resources in the planning resource pool.
  - Staff and train to supply the resources and Task Managers required by the project pipeline, including protective capacity.
- Execute:
  - Allocate resources to Task Managers for project work.
  - Measure resource performance: results and behavior.
  - Reinforce desired task manager, supervisor, and resource behavior to minimize multitasking and deliver quality task results.
  - Promptly resolve tasks escalated by Task Managers.
  - When requested by Project Managers, support buffer recovery.
- Lead continuous improvement:
  - Measure and improve the performance of Task Managers.
  - Improve the work processes for task delivery.

Task Processes

Project tasks are work processes. Resource Managers own the task work processes, and thus are accountable for task process design, execution, and improvement. Project stakeholders, including project managers, are customers for the task processes.
Resource Managers are also the subject matter experts for their technical domain, assisting project managers and senior management by providing senior level process inputs, technical oversight, process improvement, consulting, and coaching.

Execution

Resource Managers provision project tasks for execution as demanded by the statused project pipeline. They match resource availability and skill to the pipelined task needs. They provide the behavior reinforcement necessary to enable relay-racer task performance, and protect resources from interruptions and task priority changes during task execution. They play a major role in resolving the causes of stuck tasks. They assist developing and executing effective buffer recovery, including resource cross-training, realignment, overtime, etc.

Improve Processes

Resource Managers lead ongoing task estimating and performance improvement. They measure actual task performance data for future planning and execution, including developing Pareto charts and control charts of work process performance to identify effective improvement opportunities. They lead process improvement.

Behavior/Result	4	5	6	7	8	9	10	11	12	13	Wt	Raw	Points
Task manager positive reinforcements (#/day-resource)		0	.3	.5	.7	.8	1	1.2	1.5	2	20		
Tasks dispatched using task priority (avg. # demanded "red" tasks not started)		N	5	4	3	2	1	.7	.4	0	15		
Task status reported (%)	50	67	75	80	85	90	95	97	98	100	15		
Task output meets quality need (% defects)	7	6	5	4	3	2	1	0.8	0.5	0	20		
Projects perform below red region of fever chart (% of status updates in red)		50	35	25	15	10	5	4	2	0	15		
Buffer recovery actions taken on time (%)	50	67	75	80	85	90	95	97	98	100	15		

Reinforcement Plan   Total:

Points	R+ Criteria	Comments	Plans
700		5 = baseline	
850		Reinforce each movement	Verbal reinforcement in stand-up meetings.
1000		10 = full performance	Award accomplishment certificates.

Example Project Manager Performance Management Matrix: You Must Create Your Own! *Project Managers update tasks as they start and finish, and track their project weekly for review with the project team. Note that a score of 10 for all measures equals full performance, and higher scores represents outstanding. Daniels, A. and Daniels, J. (2006). Performance Management. Atlanta, GA: Performance Management Publications, p. 15*

Results	Behaviors	Reinforcements
Effective project schedule *Tasks statused* *Buffer management planned and executed* *Project issues identified and escalated if necessary* *Project actions assigned and complete* *Project change control performed* *Project risks managed*	✓ **Lead creation of effective CCPM schedule** ✓ **Enter task status daily** ✓ **Plan and execute buffer recovery as per fever chart** ✓ **Assign issues for resolution and ensure closure** ✓ **Assign actions for performance and ensure closure** ✓ **Implement project change control process** ✓ **Follow through on risks**	✓ **Verbal positive feedback on desired behaviors** ✓ **Written "thank you" upon successful project completion** ✓ **Verbal appreciation for effective buffer management** ✓ **Celebration of successful project completion**

Example Project Manager Effectiveness Measure: Project Manager's Results, Behaviors, and General Reinforcements.

Project Manager	Project Managers are responsible and accountable for all aspects of project planning and execution. The most important project manager behaviors are to **create effective Project Plans and to lead execution to that plan**. Project Management requires specific knowledge and skills. Project Managers of larger projects should be certified as Project Management Professionals (PMPs), and for smaller projects should at least have or be seeking certification as a Certified Associate in Project Management (CAPM) from the Project Management Institute. PMI. (2007). Project Manager Competency Development Framework, 2nd Edition. Newtown Square, PA: Project Management Institute

Functions	Project Managers are responsible for the following key project functions:
	➢ Project Planning:
	   o Develop all elements of a Project Plan as necessary and appropriate for the project (see module 5.6).
	   o Develop the critical chain schedule for the project, and cause it to be pipelined.
	   o Hold a project kick-off meeting with all project stakeholders to ensure buy-in to the plan.
	➢ Project Execution:
	   o Authorize task managers to start execution in accordance with prioritized task lists.
	   o Ensure effective task statusing and execution.
	   o Lead weekly buffer management meetings to ensure project flow.
	   o Manage project changes, issues, and actions, escalating to senior management as necessary to achieve the project goal.
	   o Reinforce effective behaviors on the part of all project stakeholders.
	Due to their vital role, Project Managers must be accessible at all times, or designate an alternate.

Project Plans	Develop the necessary elements of the project plan, starting with the customer's statement of work, a Work Breakdown Structure, and project planning assumptions. Develop the critical chain schedule to the WBS, ensuring that customer need dates are met as outputs from the schedule. Communicate the Project Plan to all project stakeholders before starting work on the project.
Execution	Project Managers lead project execution to the plan. Project Managers lead project meetings at least weekly to move the project along. Focus the project meeting on the statused project schedule. Assign buffer recovery and other actions as necessary for success and escalate calls for help to senior management when needed.
Continuous Improvement	Project Managers track the causes of delay or rework in their projects to effect improvements in future projects and institutionalize the improvements through company systems.

Behavior/Result	4	5	6	7	8	9	10	11	12	13	Wt	Raw	Points
Middle management LPM behavior reinforced (times/day)	1	2	3	5	6	8	10	12	16	20	20		
% escalated tasks cleared in one day	50	67	75	80	85	90	95	97	98	100	15		
Projects always work to an approved prioritized pipeline (% compliance)		0	25	50	75	85	95	97	98	100	15		
Project management decisions rely on statused schedules (# defects/qtr)		N	.9*N	.85*N	.8*N	.75*N	3	2	1	0	15		
Project WIP controlled to deliver on all client commitments (# projects in progress)		N	.9*N	.85*N	.8*N	.75*N	.75*N	.75*N	.75*N	.6*N	20		
Projects complete with less than 100% buffer penetration (% defects)	90	80	65	50	25	10	5	4	2	0	15		

Reinforcement Plan | **Total:**

Points	R+ Criteria	Comments	Plans
700		5 = baseline	
850		Reinforce each movement	Verbal reinforcement in stand-up meetings.
1000		10 = full performance	Award accomplishment certificates.

Example Senior Manager Performance Management Matrix: You Must Create Your Own! *Senior Managers track their actual performance weekly for their own use, and review monthly with their manager. Note that a score of 10 for all measures equals full performance, and higher scores represents outstanding. Daniels, A. and Daniels, J. (2006). Performance Management. Atlanta, GA: Performance Management Publications, p. 150*
N = Desired level of WIP; e.g. number of projects in process at one time.

Results	Behaviors	Reinforcements
Projects meet due dates *Projects at or under budget* *Project quality meets customer needs* *Effective behaviors reinforced* *Project help provided when needed* *Skilled resources available* *Task output quality*	✓ **Control project WIP to meet all customer commitments** ✓ **Only perform work to current project priority list** ✓ **Work to approved pipeline** ✓ **Deploy resources to prioritized task lists** ✓ **Perform effective buffer recovery** ✓ **Perform actions necessary to ensure task output quality** ✓ **Lead continuous process improvement**	✓ **Verbal positive feedback on desired behaviors.** ✓ **Written "thank you upon task completion** ✓ **Verbal appreciation for task results quality**

Example Senior Manager Effectiveness Measure: Senior Management's Results, Behaviors, and General Reinforcements.

Senior Managers

Senior Managers design, lead, and improve the organization system to deliver on all customer needs. The most important Senior Manager behaviors are to **design an effective system and positively reinforce desired behaviors by middle managers**.

Functions

Senior Managers are responsible for the following key functions:
> Design and Implement organization work process:
> - o Set the vision for the organization.
> - o Develop all elements of the "Seven S" model of business system design (see module 6.1).
> - o Implement the three rules (see module 2.1).
> - o Design and implement the work processes necessary to deliver on the vision and the three rules.
> Lead execution:
> - o Measure system performance.
> - o Make decisions and take actions necessary to satisfy customers.
> - o Prioritize all work.
> - o Control Work in Progress (WIP) to ensure maximum system throughput and quality.
> - o Reinforce desired middle manager behavior to deliver quality project results.
> - o Promptly resolve escalated tasks.
> - o Support buffer recovery.
> Continuously improve work processes:
> - o Measure and improve project delivery system performance.

Prioritize Work

Improved flow of quality project results relies on three rules (See module 2.1). The Pipelining rule requires the prioritization of all work, a task that only senior management can perform.

Control WIP

Controlling WIP (Work in Process) enables improving due date performance, project throughput, and project quality by enabling resources to focus on the right tasks. Only senior management can control WIP because work requests can come from many sources outside and inside the organization. In the beginning, the system likely has much more WIP than appropriate to function effectively. The excess WIP causes dysfunctional behavior, such as multitasking and frequent priority switching, leading to late delivery, cost over-runs, low throughput, and poor quality. Senior management must take decisive action to reduce this WIP or system results will not improve. Whether they do this by "freezing" projects or pipelining, they must stop work on some projects and/or non-project work in order to complete all projects sooner and establish new organizational norms of project delivery. Then, they must control input to match system delivery capacity.

Improve Processes

Senior Managers lead ongoing project estimating and delivery process improvement. They measure actual project performance data for future planning and execution, and use Six Sigma and Lean tools such as Pareto charts and control charts to identify effective improvement opportunities. They lead the overall process improvement.

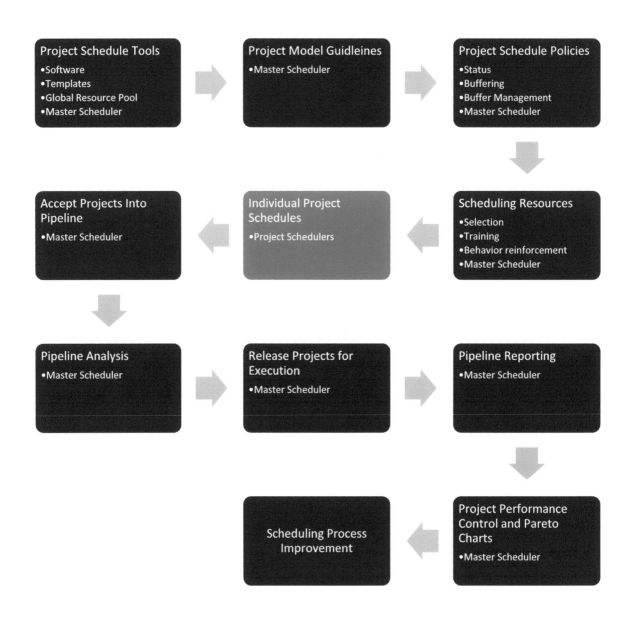

Project Scheduling Process. Purple process steps illustrate key master scheduler roles.

6.6 Master Scheduler

Summary

The Master Scheduler acts as the process owner for project scheduling and for developing and maintaining the project pipeline. He or she also acts as the senior subject matter expert for scheduling across the organization. The PMI project manager competency guide describes many of the competencies that the Master Scheduler must possess.

PMI. (2007). Project Manager Competency Development Framework, 2nd Edition. Newtown Square, PA: Project Management Institute

Functions

The scheduling process owner functions include:
- ➢ Process Design.
- ➢ User training.
- ➢ Maintenance.
- ➢ Operation.
- ➢ Improvement.

The scheduling subject matter expert functions include for all of the schedulers in the organization:
- ➢ Acquiring.
- ➢ Training.
- ➢ Providing input for performance development.

The Master Scheduler also operates the pipelining function, including:
- ➢ Maintain the project priority list.
- ➢ Add, delete, or modify projects in the pipeline.
- ➢ Perform "what if" analyses of enterprise scheduling alternatives.
- ➢ Establish the start date for projects.

PMI. (2007). Practice Standard for Scheduling. Newtown Square, PA: Project Management Institute

Knowledge Areas

- ➢ Work Breakdown Structure.
- ➢ Network Development.
- ➢ Estimating.
- ➢ CCPM, including:
  - o Resource loading and leveling of project schedules.
  - o Buffer types and sizing practices.
  - o Pipelining.
  - o Buffer Management.
- ➢ Project Status and Reporting.
- ➢ Scheduling Software.
- ➢ Process Improvement Methodologies (e.g. Six Sigma, Lean).

Qualifications

Master Schedulers should be subject matter experts in project and program management. They should be certified as PMI Scheduling Professionals (PMI-SP), Project Management Professionals (PMP), or equivalent. They must be skilled in the application of the organization's scheduling tools and stay abreast of knowledge in the field of project and program schedule management.

Master Schedulers must have written and oral communication capabilities and be proficient with common office software such as email, word processing, spreadsheets, and graphics. They should also have knowledge of how to establish and operate collaboration tools, such as SharePoint sites or Wikis.

Behavior/Result	4	5	6	7	8	9	10	11	12	13	Wt	Raw	Points
Tasks started using task priority (# demanded "red" tasks not started)		N					1			0	20		
Task status reported (%)	50	67	75	80	85	90	95	97	98	100	20		
Tasks completed using relay racer performance (# of open tasks at any one time)		3		2			1	1	1	1	20		
Task output meets quality need (% defects)	7	6	5	4	3	2	1	0.8	0.5	0	20		
Stuck tasks escalated within 24 hours (%)	50	67	75	80	85	90	95	97	98	100	20		

Reinforcement Plan			Total:	
Points	**R+ Criteria**	**Comments**	**Plans**	
700		5 = baseline		
850		Reinforce each movement	Verbal reinforcement in stand-up meetings.	
1000		10 = full performance	Award accomplishment certificates.	

Example Performing Resource Performance Management Matrix: You Must Create Your Own!

Performing resources do the work. Note that a score of 10 for all measures equals' full performance, and higher scores represents outstanding. When the blocks are empty, use the closest numbered entry. Daniels, A. and Daniels, J. (2006). Performance Management. Atlanta, GA: Performance Management Publications, p. 15

Results	Behaviors	Reinforcements
Tasks started according to task priority *Task status reported to Task Manager* *Tasks completed applying relay-racer performance* *Stuck tasks escalated*	✓ **Work on their highest priority task.** ✓ **Focus on one task at a time.** ✓ **Perform actions necessary to ensure task output quality.** ✓ **Complete one task before starting another, even if a non-working task climbs to higher priority.** ✓ **Request help immediately if task delayed.** ✓ **Report task status to the Task Manager.**	✓ **Verbal positive feedback on desired behaviors.** ✓ **Written "thank you" upon task completion.** ✓ **Verbal appreciation for task results quality.**

Example Performing Resource Effectiveness Measures and General Reinforcements.

Performing Resource

Performing resources do the work on tasks to produce quality task output and pass it on to the next Task Manager (successor task) as soon as possible. They report status on their work, and generate calls for management help (escalate) when a task gets stuck.

Relay Racer

Performing resources focus on one task at a time, completing it before moving on to their next task. Relay racers are the model for expected behavior: get the baton (task input) as soon as possible for your leg of the race, perform your part of the race as quickly as you can, while ensuring the quality of the task output, and smoothly pass on the result to the next racer (task manager) in the chain of tasks.

Seamless handoff of the results to the next task performer is vital. Did you see the two potentially winning teams in the Beijing Olympics lose their races by dropping the baton at the handoff?

Task Status

Performing resources must help ensure timely and accurate task status information. Your task status information can affect the task priority for all resources on all projects.

Status tasks with the actual start date when you start them, the actual completion date when you finish them, and with an estimate of remaining duration at least once a week*, on the standard status day for the project. (The standard status day for the project is the day before the project meeting). The mechanism to put task performer status input into the schedule depends on your software and update process.

Use your knowledge and skill with similar tasks in the past and your knowledge of the current situation to estimate remaining duration (RDU) for your tasks. Keep in mind that the remaining duration estimates is in standard work days; you should not add non-working days such as weekends or holidays into your estimate for remaining duration. If you have to make assumptions to make your estimate, make them clear to the task manager.

Very short duration projects may require a higher standard update frequency; e.g. every day or even every shift.

Escalation

Escalate your task for management help immediately if you are stuck; e.g. need task inputs or management decisions. You can expect immediate help if your task is causing the buffer to be in the red and timely help in any case. Do not wait until the scheduled status or next meeting to escalate! Do it as soon as you become aware of the problem.

7. Leading Change

The greatest challenge most managers face is to lead effective change within their own organization. The body of organizational change literature attests to the difficulty of the challenge, and offers a host of remedies. If there is a common thread to the literature, it is that effective change is always harder and takes much longer to accomplish than expected.

The Theory of Constraints offers an approach to causing change deploying the "layers of resistance" model, first proposed by Goldratt, and later extended by others. It is a very convincing logical model. I tried using the model on some early implementations of CCPM and found it of little value. I am willing to accept that perhaps it was my faulty use of it that led to less than stellar results. At the same time, I was deeply engaged in the study of psychology and the organizational change literature. These studies led me to clarify a number of shortcomings in the layers of resistance model, including:

1. It has no basis in theory, and no scientific testing of validity. It is simply a proposition.
2. It is a purely cognitive model. Organization change is about changing behavior.
3. It addresses individuals, not the social aspects of organizations.

Those considerations caused me to move on in search of a better model.

I discovered the work of John Kotter early in my studies of organizational change. It specifically deals with the issues that were not working for me with the TOC model, and did have a substantial basis of research and testing behind it. The approach described in this section closely follows his recommendations. It works, if used. It isn't easy to get leadership teams to rigorously follow the approach of the model. When they do so, implementing change happens much faster and produces greater and more lasting success.

There is one key aspect of successful change leadership that I do not think Kotter emphasizes enough. Case studies of dozens of CCPM/LPM implementations show one common strong thread. If the organizational leader makes the change his or her top priority, it will be accomplished quickly with little pain, and deliver huge rewards. If the organization leader is uninvolved on a daily basis, implementation will drag on and deliver minimal results. If the organization leader delegates the implementation of process improvement, even if delegated to strong individuals, little will happen. On the other hand, if the changed behavior becomes the agenda of the organization leader, change happens with little ado.

I recently had dinner with the leader of CCPM in a large, very successful company. He described a company in which CCPM was the way the company did business. Every morning, the first thing the CEO of the company did was to have a short meeting with his direct reports to review the multiproject fever charts for all of their ongoing projects, both new plants and major customer projects. They focused on the projects that needed their help, and left the meeting with decisions made and actions assigned. A new client that was with me asked, "How do you deal with suppliers that do not do CCPM?" The leader answered, "We ask them to use CCPM". My new client followed up with, "How do you get them to do so?" The leader answered, "We ask them if they want our business. Sometimes our CEO has to visit their CEO. All our suppliers use CCPM, and feed into our projects via feeding buffers." Get the picture?

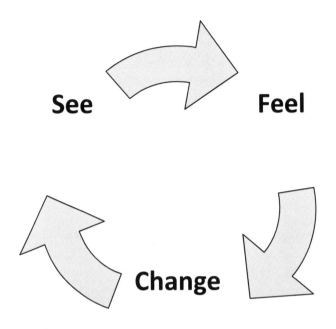

Leading Organization Change Is An Ongoing Leadership Process. *Coaching a team to new levels of performance may describe it best. Emotion (feel) drives change...towards a vision you can see.*

Eight Steps to Effectively Lead Organization Change Initiatives. *Although not evident from this depiction, step 8 takes you back to step 1. The colored circles represent four stages: 1- Set the stage, 2- Decide what to do, 3- Make it happen, and 4- Make it stick.*

Lead!	Leading organization change requires focused leadership. Organizations are designed to produce stable repeatable performance. What people do…behavior…causes organization results. Your organization is perfectly designed to produce all of the results it currently achieves, both successes and failures. Research demonstrates that organization change begins with establishing an emotional need…a sense of urgency to bring about change. Without that urgency, fear, anger, other emotions and existing behavior reinforcements ensure that the organization will not change for the better. The figure on the lower left illustrates the eight steps for effective change leadership developed and tested by Kotter and Cohen. I have found their model to be most effective. Kotter, J. and Cohen, S. (2002). *The Heart of Change.* Boston: Harvard Business School Press Cohen, D.(2005). The Heart of Change Field Guide. Boston: Harvard Business School Press
Establish the Need	Leadership teams must first establish a sense of urgency to make a change, and maintain a sense of urgency to continuously improve. Without a sense of urgency to continuously improve, organization behavior will not change, or will revert to past behavior as soon as a crisis ensues. A sense of urgency aligns all of the organization thought leaders to "go for it!" It makes the change the first item on their daily agendas. To that end, the team that leads the change must be the thought leaders of the organization.
Set the Direction	Begin with the end mind. Please review step 8 (module 7.9) before developing your implementation plan. The Vision and Communicate steps develop and communicate a Vision of the changed organization to enlist everyone that must change behavior to achieve the new results. Lean and Critical Chain Project Management demand some non-intuitive behaviors that people in the organization have not experienced before. They need to know the expected behaviors and be led to build skill in performing them.
Coach	The Empower and Short-term wins steps coach people through the changes. Management must empower people to try the new behaviors, providing reinforcing feedback as they improve their skills. Communicating the short-term accomplishments across the organization builds confidence and skill to apply the new behaviors and achieve ever-improving skill.
Make it Last	The final steps ensure that the changed behaviors become the starting point for additional improvement. There will be times that the new behaviors are challenging and the next improvement step seems daunting. That's where leadership must demonstrate its ability to coach and lead. Once the organization reaches the initial performance goals it's time to examine and plan the next improvement to assure the long-term persistence of the gains accomplished.

The Case for Change Comes from *What Is* versus *What Needs to Be*. *Data on performance gaps, errors, unhappy customers, competition, market trends, and so forth can help you find and make the case for change, and identify reasons for the complacency that allows the gaps to persist.*

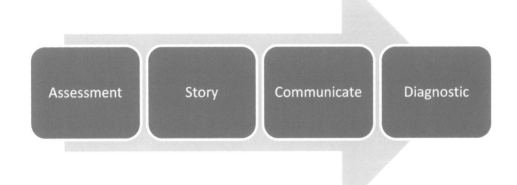

A Process to Develop and Implement Your Sense of Urgency. *See Cohen.*

Urgency	People have to believe that there is a reason to change what they are doing. They need to visualize the gap between current and future performance and what is needed to overcome complacency with the present situation. Kotter and Cohen's research demonstrates that rational business cases do not cause change. Stories and images that engage our emotions create the energy necessary to make the change. Kotter, J. and Cohen, S. (2002). *The Heart of Change*. Boston: Harvard Business School Press, pp. 1-36 Cohen, D. (2005). The Heart of Change Field Guide. Boston: Harvard Business School Press, pp. 13-33
See -> Feel -> Change	Some change advocates recommend analysis; think through what is needed, and then cause "buy-in". Research demonstrates that such logic-based approaches rarely lead to effective lasting change. Emotive visual images and stories motivate change.
Alligators In The Yard	Organizations sometimes are in such a crisis mode that they have to focus on the immediate problems before they can get on with any kind of improvement. If there are alligators in your backyard, you need to move them on before you start planting your garden. But, as soon as they are out of the way, you are ready to plant the seeds for the future. That's when communicating WHY we need to do something different for our long-term good must take over.
Everyone	Urgency must make sense to everyone. It won't impact all to the same degree, but they have to be engaged enough to subordinate other things to the sense of urgency to get on with the change. Current work processes already take up all peoples' available time. Where is the incremental effort necessary to bring about any kind of change going to come from? People will change when they feel that the benefits outweigh the temporary need to develop and deploy some new systems or behaviors.
What's Your Story?	Your organization must find the compelling story that will work for you. Some of the following may relate to your organization's urgency for change: • Everyone is fed up with the constantly changing task priorities. • Hugely detailed plans and procedures never happen. • Few use the detailed plans for anything. • People leave work each day exhausted and wondering if anything useful was accomplished. • Various parts of the organization are constantly blaming others for not delivering what they need for their work. • If you don't change, your company will be out of business and you will be out of a job. Whatever the driver, you need to put it into a form everyone can relate to. Pictures (including videos) are truly worth a thousand words for this purpose, but putting 150 words into a compelling story are also worth more than 1,000 words or a 1,000 cell spreadsheet making a logical business case for change. What's your story?

Plan
- Appoint a Project Manager
- Develop the implementation plan
- Assure resources

Organize
- Assign team responsibilities
- Appoint subordinate teams

Lead
- Set implementation project vision and goals
- Communicate and solicit feedback from the organization
- Make decisions
- Dissolve conflicts between people or organizations

Control
- Measure performance to goals and implemention plan
- Manage implementation project buffer
- Resolve technical issues

Characteristics of a Strong Guiding Team. *The guiding team can use measures like these and pp. 48 & 57 of Cohen to set goals and guide their performance. After Cohen, p. 48*

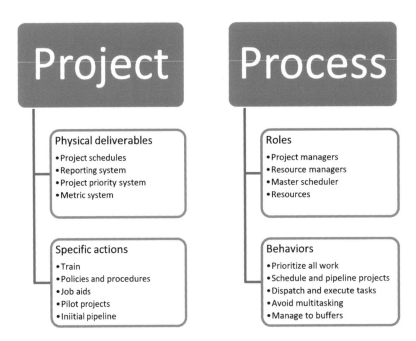

Project

Physical deliverables
- Project schedules
- Reporting system
- Project priority system
- Metric system

Specific actions
- Train
- Policies and procedures
- Job aids
- Pilot projects
- Iniitial pipeline

Process

Roles
- Project managers
- Resource managers
- Master scheduler
- Resources

Behaviors
- Prioritize all work
- Schedule and pipeline projects
- Dispatch and execute tasks
- Avoid multitasking
- Manage to buffers

The Guiding Team Leads Both a Project and a Process Improvement. *They first have to form themselves into an effective team.*

Guiding Team

The guiding team is the internal leadership team to cause the change. They report to the change sponsor. It is not the entire leadership team of the organization, but a small enough group to act as an effective team to bring about the necessary results. Collectively the team members possess all the skills necessary to lead the change, including the ability to quickly form into an effective team themselves. The guiding team members are willing and able to devote the necessary time and effort to bring about the organizational results as quickly and seamlessly as possible.

Kotter, J. and Cohen, S. (2002). *The Heart of Change*. Boston: Harvard Business School Press, pp. 37-60
Cohen, D. (2005). *The Heart of Change Field Guide*. Boston: Harvard Business School Press, pp. 35-61

Purpose

The guiding team's purpose is to bring the LPM benefits to the organization as soon as possible such that they will endure into the future. While a project manager should report to the guiding team to plan and execute the discrete steps necessary to bring about the change, the guiding team must cause the necessary changes in behavior; i.e. organization work processes, such as pipelining.

Team Goals

All new teams go through a predictable process of forming, norming, and storming before performing. Setting lofty team goals at the outset helps move through this process. The team goals should be "SMART": specific, measurable, agreed upon, responsibility assigned and timely (i.e. have a firm completion date). The team needs to address how they are progressing towards those goals on an ongoing basis.

Organizational Trust

The guiding team must develop and maintain the trust of members of the organization that they are there to make the change work as effectively as possible to bring benefits to everyone. Guiding team members solicit feedback from the organization and act on it.

Team Process

The guiding team must lead:
  ➢ Set the standard for effective teamwork.
  ➢ Use an agenda and publish minutes and action lists.
  ➢ Assign and perform actions and resolve issues and actions.
  ➢ Remove roadblocks for implementers.
  ➢ Assure that the implementation work is synchronized.
  ➢ Set the example for LPM by using a CCPM plan for the project part of the implementation.
  ➢ Use metrics and feedback control for the process parts of the implementation.
  ➢ Provide positive reinforcement of desired behaviors.

Feedback

The guiding team members use ongoing feedback to improve the implementation process. While formal measures provide information they can use as feedback, they are both communicators and solicitors of direct feedback from the organization on how it is going. In the beginning, soliciting this type of feedback may not come naturally to all of the guiding team members, so they will need to help each other.

Seeing
- PICTURE of the FUTURE STATE
- In the PRESENT tense: WE ARE...

Feeling (Emotions)
- Escape from negative: Frustration, Anger, Anxiety
- Link to positive: Happiness, Pride, Security, Serenity
- STORIES work best!

Changing
- Daily topic
- Positive talk (vs. skeptical or cynical: we SHALL overcome!)
- Link, feedback, and reinforce behaviors that make it so.

The Organization Must Share a Vision. *A Vision is a mental snapshot of where the organization is going, but in the present tense; as if it were already there.*

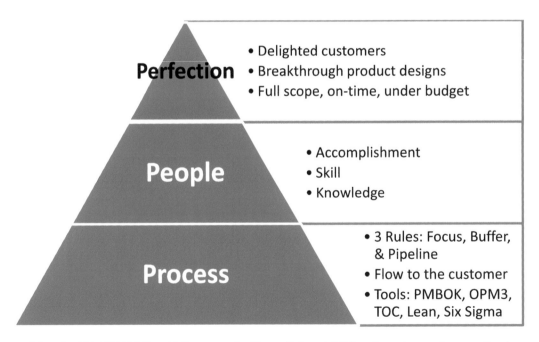

Perfection
- Delighted customers
- Breakthrough product designs
- Full scope, on-time, under budget

People
- Accomplishment
- Skill
- Knowledge

Process
- 3 Rules: Focus, Buffer, & Pipeline
- Flow to the customer
- Tools: PMBOK, OPM3, TOC, Lean, Six Sigma

A Vision for LPM/CCPM Should Focus on the Three Rules. *Additional requirements or methods can come from the business improvement methods.*

Vision

The vision sets a clear direction by describing the destination…as if you are already there. Think about the vision as the cover on your organization's travel brochure…white sands, blue ocean, green palm trees, the breeze blowing the hair of two beautiful people smiling at you.

A vision must be short, simple, and inspiring; "We delight our customers by delivering more than they expected, on-time, all the time."

Development

Think about what it takes to inspire you to commit to something significant in your life: going to college, getting married, having children, buying a new house, taking a new job, learning a new hobby. You need a picture in your mind of the end state that triggers your emotions to desire it. That's a vision.

The vision must be:
- ➢ **Inspiring**: something more than we are today.
- ➢ **Compelling**.
- ➢ **Desirable**: something everyone would want to be part of.
- ➢ **Realistic**: something we can sign on to create.
- ➢ **Clear:** understood pretty much the same by everybody.
- ➢ **Focused**: discriminates us from others; what we do vs. don't do.
- ➢ **Flexible**: robust in view of what the future might bring.
- ➢ **Tangible**: everyone is able to feel the benefits of achieving it.

The management must lead the team to both develop and share the vision. Management can't bring it down from a mountain retreat. Instead, they must live with the people and learn how to develop a vision that meets everyone's desires.

For more ambitious change efforts, Dettmer's *Strategic Navigation* provides a unique set of tools to develop a vision and attainment plan.

Dettmer, W. (2003). Strategic Navigation. Milwaukee, WN: ASQ Press

Communication

Although they are not bad things to do, posting the vision on the bulletin boards, articles in the company newsletter, and fancy annual report pictures and statements do not cut it. Having your recorded message play to anyone who calls your business doesn't cut it, especially if your employees don't know what the message is saying.

Everyone must see the vision in action: actually influencing what people do. If it does not come up in every meeting, it should help make decisions in at least every other meeting.

Feedback

Acquire and act positively on feedback. Measure trends in:
- ➢ Knowing what the vision is.
- ➢ Understanding how the vision "relates to me".
- ➢ Agreement that "I have to work to keep the vision."
- ➢ Belief that the vision is achievable.
- ➢ Agreement that others in the organization share the vision.

Continuously improve understanding of the vision, communication, and the vision itself as necessary to lead and coach the organization to deliver their best.

Create Urgency	Cause the change	Sustain the change
•Why make a change...the emotional benefits. •The direction of change: strategy and tactics to achieve the benefits. •The vision.	•Clarify behaviors. •Reinforce behaviors. •Obtain feedback and adapt.	•Consolidate learning. •Institutionalize processes. •Continuously improve.

Communication Content Changes With Time. *It starts with the need for change, and ends with beginning the next major improvement direction.*

Row	Stakeholder	Action	Key Message	Due Date	Media	Responsibility			Status
						Develop	Review Approve	Deliver	
1	Performing resources	Task work	When to start	Weekly	Schedule software	TM	PM	Intranet	OK
2	Task Managers	Dispatch tasks; escalate help needs	When to start tasks Escalation	Weekly	Schedule software, Project Meeting	TM	PM	MS	OK
3	Project sponser	Decisions	Project status and issues	Monthly	Project report, SharePoint site	PM	SP	TM	OK
4	Users	Test and use product	Benefits, Features, How to use	3 mo. Prior to roll out	Emails, training sessions	PM	SP	TM	Not started
5	Suppliers	Deliver inputs	Specifications, delivery needs	Before and during contract	Email, Telephone, Mail	TM	PM	TM	Not started
6	Senior Management	Decisions, actions to resolve issues	Status, Help needs	Monthly, as needed for escalated tasks	Telephone, Email, Meeting	PM	SP	PM	OK
PM: Project Manager TM: Task Manager SM: Senior Management					SP: Project Sponser MS: Master Scheduler				

Communication Plan Template. *As with all plans, the communication plan specifies why, what, who, when, and how.*

Purpose Communication to implement a new vision is a multi-objective multi-directional, ongoing process. You cannot communicate too much. Most organizations that fail to successfully implement change, or just take much longer than necessary to achieve the benefits, fail on communication.

Stakeholders Communication considers the needs of all project delivery system stakeholders: past, present, and future. You need to assess and prioritize your stakeholders and the messages that must be sent and received. It helps to initially assess where the stakeholders are on the need for and direction of change to prioritize where you need to take them. Communication implies a two-direction interchange to verify that the necessary messages have been transmitted and that the content has been understood as intended.

Communication Plan The communication plan specifies what each stakeholder needs, how their needs will be met, and who will do it. The template on the left indicates the key fields to consider in your communication plan. Once you have developed the overall communication plan, you can include the specific actions necessary to implement it in your project schedule and/or project action system. Include repetitive actions in your project plan, using the due date column to specify the frequency.

The following provides some ideas for communication media:

Face-to-face meetings	Magazines	Teleconferencing and voice
Group meetings	Intranet	messaging
One-on-one	Executive presentations	Posters and banners
communications	Training and workshops	Memos and letters
Email	Project team presentations	Update bulletins
Newsletters	Stand-up meetings	Special social events
Television	Artifacts	Flyers and circulars
Radio	Shirts, hats, etc. LCD/plasma	Video conferencing
Demonstrations	screen displays	Videotapes

An implementer of Lean in organizations commented that, "If you want organizations to do things differently, you have to communicate everything at least six times and at least three different ways". People respond differently to media. One key classification is sensory: visual, aural, and kinesthetic. Other classifications address temperaments. Consider the variety of the individuals in your stakeholder groups as you communicate.

Feedback Acquire and act positively on feedback. Measure trends in:
  ➢ Knowing what the change is
  ➢ Understanding how the change "relates to me"
  ➢ Agreement that "I have to work to make the change"
  ➢ Belief that the change is achievable
  ➢ Agreement that others in the organization share making the change
Although these questions parallel the vision questions, the scope is much broader, including all elements of the change. After the initial communication of urgency, vision, and necessary knowledge, the larger part of the communication focus feeds back short-term wins to reinforce necessary behaviors by all stakeholders.

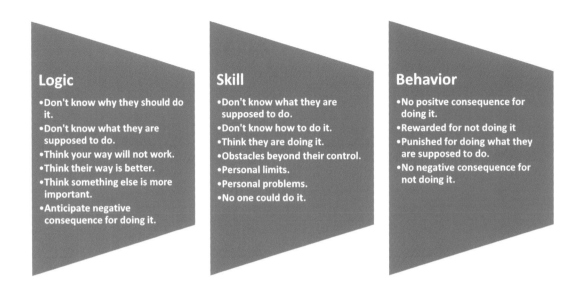

Many Potential Barriers Challenge Enablement. *Implementation needs to focus on the key stakeholders: senior and mid-level managers. After Fournies.*

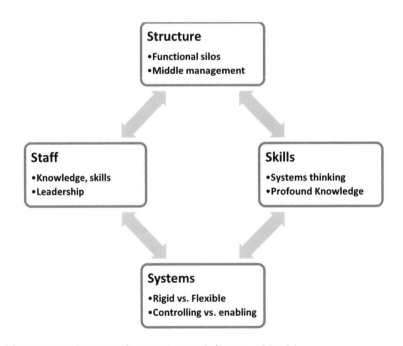

Major Enablement Barriers. *For diagnostic, see Cohen, p. 132-134*

Purpose   Enable all stakeholders to move to desired behaviors by removing obstacles, reinforcing the desired behaviors (modules 6.1 and 6.2), and removing reinforcements for the undesired behaviors.

Diagnostic   Before you can determine how to cause the changes in behavior needed to reach the vision, you have to know where people are. Develop and deploy a diagnostic tool following that proposed by Cohen (132-134) to track progress.
Cohen, D. (2005). The Heart of Change Field Guide. Boston, MA: Harvard Business School Press.

Barriers   Barriers can exist in any of the Seven S dimensions (module 6.1). The most significant usually are Systems, Skills, and Structure.
  - Systems
    o   People are safe to take risks and make mistakes
    o   Performance criteria match desired behaviors
      ▪   Performance Appraisals
      ▪   Pay
      ▪   Hiring
    o   Promotions support change leaders
  - Skills
  - Structure
    o   Accountability for cross-functional processes
    o   Shared priority
    o   Align authority with responsibility

The most important underlying barrier is fear. People, and particularly managers, have been reinforced to exhibit the behaviors they practice today. Changing those behaviors requires reinforcing the desired behavior and removing the reinforcers for the undesired behavior. They have not experienced reinforcement for the new behaviors. Changing our own behavior is often problematic. Consider how many people sincerely desire to lose weight or stop smoking yet are unable to do so. In some cases, as documented by a study of heart patients in *"Change or Die"*, the urgency to change is as serious as it can get. The vision is clear. They have received communications. Yet, they fail.

Fournies documented many potential causes for apparent "resistance" to change. Consider these relative to the managers in your organization as you seek to empower them to act.
Deutschman, A. (2007). Change or Die. Los Angeles, CA: Regan
Fournies, F. (1988). Why Employees Don't Do What They're Supposed to Do. Liberty Hall Press.

Feedback   Acquire and act positively on feedback. Measure trends in:
  - Leadership "walking the talk".
  - Stakeholders practicing the desired behavior (6.1 to 6.7).
  - Positive vs. negative feedback on the change.
  - Agreement that "I have to work to make the change."
  - Improvements in the diagnostic measures.
  - Improvements in results.

Psychological research demonstrates that resistance to change comes from emotions (most often: fear). The resistance is not a conscious decision, and is therefore not necessarily "rational". Nonetheless, if challenged people will confabulate reasons for doing things that do not support the desired change. Your best strategy is to watch what they actually do and plan and execute your change leadership actions from that "feedback".

Plan Short-term Wins

- Select projects, prototypes, and/or key events or results.
  - Measurable
  - Visible
  - Timely
  - Relevant to:
    - Stakeholders
    - Objectives
    - Situation
    - People
- Schedule to achieve continuous flow of wins.
- Assign actions.
- Communicate expectations.

Execute Projects

- Coach those generating wins.
- Remove obstacles for prototype teams.
- Use temporary methods when needed.
- Reinforce the teams creating the wins.

Analyze, Communicate and Act

- Evaluate the results of your expected short-term wins.
- Communicate the wins.
- Assess the effect of communication.
- Adjust both your changes and your communication.

Plan and Create Short-term-wins. *Short-term wins should start within a month of kicking off the implementation, and flow at least monthly until the system is operational..*

#	Desired Outcome	Key Measures	Communication Media	Actions	Due Date	Responsibility
1						
2						
3						
4						
5						
6						
7						
8						
9						
10						

Short-term Wins Planning Tool. *As with all plans, specify what, who, when, where, and how. Transfer the actions to your action tracking system or implementation project plan.*

Purpose   Creating and communicating short-terms wins reinforces the direction of change. Key success factors include the frequency and credibility of the results achieved and how the organization perceives them. Effective communication of frequent positive results provides the force to increase change momentum. Wins provide positive, immediate, and certain reinforcement for the desired new behaviors.

    ➤ Feedback to the change leaders on the validity of the vision, strategy, and tactics.
    ➤ Emotional uplift.
    ➤ Recruitment of those who are not yet aboard for the journey.
    ➤ Disempowerment of change cynics.

You cannot do without short-term wins…they propel the change!

Planning   If your change delivers the results you expect, wins will happen. They are too important to the momentum for change to leave them to chance. Develop a specific list of wins, plan to accomplish them and then reward, celebrate and communicate achieving them. Prototype projects should be part of your plan, but not the complete plan.

Plan prototype projects with care, ensuring that you specify and communicate that the objective of prototypes is to find out what elements of your organization must change to align with the direction of LPM/CCPM.

Prototype   Prototype or pilot projects are a powerful means to generate short-term wins. Consider them like the continuous improvement cycles of Six Sigma: prototype projects, enabling tests for how to best align improvement with your environment. Analysis of the prototypes helps you tailor the system-wide roll out to include improvements identified during the prototype.

LPM/CCPM prototypes can start with single projects, but in most cases single projects will not show as much gain as multiproject prototypes. The reason is that most of the gain comes from eliminating multitasking, and single projects often entail more limited multitasking to start with. Try to select small groups of small projects that share common resources.

Select your prototypes with care. The prototype leaders should be strong advocates of the change. They must understand the vision.

Diagnostic   You can plan for short terms wins that seem valuable, but how they impact the organization may not match your expectations. You need to solicit feedback, and adjust your plan as necessary to achieve the desired result. Develop and deploy a diagnostic tool following that proposed by Cohen (151-153) to track progress.

Cohen, D. (2005). The Heart of Change Field Guide. Boston, MA: Harvard Business School Press.

Feedback   Solicit feedback from those who most support the change, those who most resist it, and those in between. The latter are the most important to focus communicating wins to. Determine the effectiveness of the wins themselves, and the effectiveness of the communication on them. Be alert for "spin" on the communications.

Wins in one part of the organization do not automatically transfer to other parts of an organization. Expect initial feedback to suggest that the wins "won't work here" because "they cheated", or "they were so bad, anything would have helped", and so on. The answer is to forge on and create more and more wins.

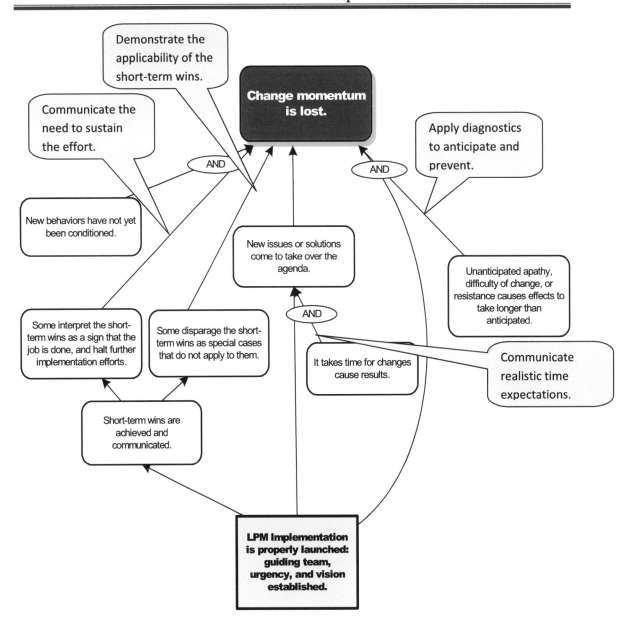

Negative Branch, a TOC Tool, Describes Potential Causes of Momentum Loss. *Read the tree from the bottom up, "IF x, AND IF y, then z". For example, the lower right branch, "IF LPM Implementation is properly launched: guiding team, urgency, and vision established, AND IF unanticipated apathy, difficulty of change, or resistance causes effects to take longer than anticipated, THEN change momentum is lost". Focus prevention where it turns negative, as indicated by the callouts.*

Purpose   Sustain the urgency and momentum of the change to LPM/CCPM despite the tendency to let up following initial wins or give up if it seems to be taking more effort or a longer time to get results than initially expected. Attaining large results always takes longer than people think it should.

Symptoms   In the time of sailing ships from Europe to America, the favored route took ships through pretty good sailing for most of the way from Europe, but often took them to an area of calm winds near the equator, best described by Coleridge in The Rime of the Ancient Mariner:

> *Day after day, day after day,*
> *We stuck, nor breath nor motion;*
> *As idle as a painted ship*
> *Upon a painted ocean.*

Almost all change initiatives run into their doldrums. You can sail into them from the north or the south: you get early great results, so people want to "bask in the glory", or you encounter resistance, and some begin to feel "it's too hard". Symptoms include:

- ➤ Planned changes are not getting done.
- ➤ Issues identified for action are ignored.
- ➤ Key leaders unavailable for meetings.
- ➤ Recommendations shelved.
- ➤ Decisions recycled.
- ➤ Resources committed elsewhere.

If these are happening to your project, you are in the doldrums.

Solutions   Potential solutions include:

- ➤ Understand that change is more than managing the implementation project plan.
- ➤ Assess progress of change, and act when your buffer is in the red!
- ➤ Create processes for ongoing accountability.
- ➤ Change measurement system to drive behavior.
- ➤ Change measurement system to drive results.
- ➤ Perform corrective action.
- ➤ Sustain sponsorship.
- ➤ Reinforce desired behaviors.
- ➤ Link the changes to the organization's culture and value system.

Diagnostic   Develop and deploy a diagnostic tool following that proposed by Cohen (178-179) to track progress.

Cohen, D. (2005). The Heart of Change Field Guide. Boston, MA: Harvard Business School Press.

Feedback   Solicit feedback from those who most support the change, those who most resist it, and those in between. The latter are the most important to focus your continuing efforts to change. Determine the effectiveness of the changes and the effectiveness of all of your change efforts.

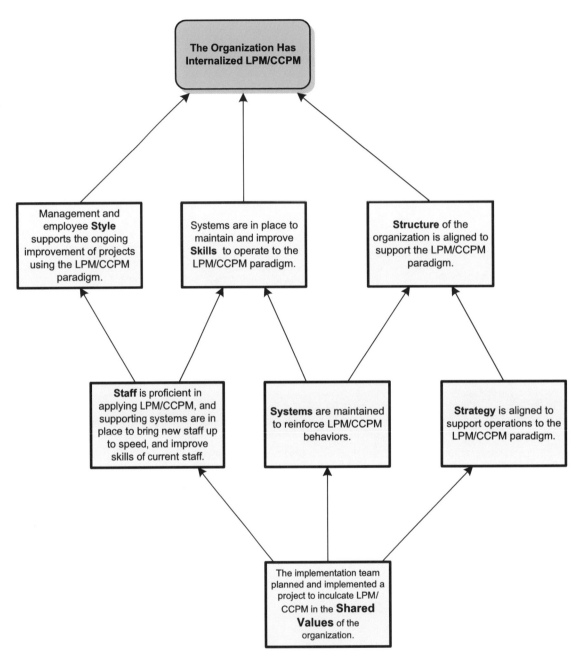

Intermediate Objective Map Illustrates How Seven Ss Work to Create Desired Effect. *Read this tree from the top down, "In order to have <entity at the head of the arrow> we must first have <entity at the tail of the arrow>". Build your implementation plan to achieve these intermediate objectives, and use a diagnostic tool to assure ongoing maintenance of the desired effect.*

Purpose

The final step in implementing change sets the change in the DNA of the organization, establishing a new baseline for future improvements. This road never ends.

Embed the Changes in the Organizational DNA

The seven S model introduced in module 6.1, provides a holistic view of the organization. The figure illustrates one view of strong relationships between the Seven S elements. In reality, each element connects to all the other elements, feeding back success in one element to another. The elements that must be firmly established for a new baseline to persist include:

> **Shared Values and Vision**: overt and subtle expressions of the organizational values and vision demonstrate that LPM/CCPM are "the way we do business around here".

> **Systems**: management systems, including policies, procedures, IT infrastructure, and human resource systems align with and support the shared values and vision.

> **Structure**: organizational structure aligns with the project flow paradigm.

> **Strategy**: organizational strategy builds on the new capacity, and uses the TOC, Six Sigma, and Lean tools to build new throughput enhancing strategies for the future.

> **Staff**: staff are hired, trained, and sustained with the ability to perform to the Lean system and continuous improvement values of the organization.

> **Style**: supportive management style continues to improve the organization design. Managers act as mentors and coaches to enhance the flow of projects that support the strategy to attain the shared vision.

> **Skills**: employee skills are continually enhanced to better perform both the operational and system improvement tasks that lie ahead.

The relationships between the Ss are as important as the entities themselves.

Diagnostic

Develop and deploy a diagnostic tool following that proposed by Cohen (198-199) to establish additional reinforcements needed.

Cohen, D. (2005). The Heart of Change Field Guide. Boston, MA: Harvard Business School Press.

Feedback

Solicit feedback from those who most supported the change, those who most resisted it, and those in between. The resistors are key to establishing if this change has been assimilated, and you are ready for the next round.

The End?

The best way to ensure that the organization does not return to its previous mode of operation is to set ever higher goals, seeking the Lean goal of perfection. Stability is one point on an infinite curve between degradation towards death and continuous unending improvement. Improvement may be one of very few things that appear to not have a constraint, as long you continue to follow the TOC five focusing steps and Lean-Sigma approaches to improve forever.

8. Networks

I learned to develop and use project schedule networks early in my career, and quickly came to expect them as a norm. With few exceptions, the projects and organizations I worked with either had or were able to easily create networks of the tasks necessary for their projects. I didn't realize it at the time, but one reason they were able to do so is that they were all driven to first create Work Breakdown Structures (WBS) by their budgeting systems. The WBS naturally subdivided the work, easing network development.

When I first went into consulting, it was with clients dominated by government projects similar to those in my previous work, and although I found a bit more difficulties with the project networks, they generally required only modest improvements to make effective schedules. As I expanded my consulting practice, I found the practice I had been exposed to was the exception, not the norm. Most businesses were not acquainted with the WBS or task networks. Their idea of a project schedule was a list of tasks with dates. I was appalled at the confusing lists of tasks people would try to use to run projects. I also found that initial attempts to teach people to use the WBS were met with great resistance, and that some people had great difficulty arranging the project deliverables using a WBS.

I wish I could say I found the secret to helping those who have difficulty with creating a WBS. Instead, I have encouraged the people who are WBS challenged to have someone able to do it create their WBS for them, or I sit them down and do it with them in an hour or so for the largest projects. Once an organization has created WBSs for their typical projects, most people can add to them or subtract from them to get an effective WBS for their project.

Three additional things that I have found to have great value for projects, and which are almost never practiced outside certain industries, are:
1. To write down the assumptions necessary to define the project (i.e. while creating the WBS), and to develop the project schedule.
2. For larger projects, to create a Milestone Sequence Chart, laying out the major sequence of the work, before beginning to create the network of tasks.
3. Also for larger projects, to use the "Work Package" concept to develop small networks for the major project deliverables, and link them using the Milestone Sequence Chart.

Later, I found that these practices were quite familiar to those in the "projects for profit" businesses; i.e. companies that manage large projects as their business such as large construction and aerospace companies.

Many of the people that teach Critical Chain come from a production background, and are not familiar with these project disciplines. I was astonished early on to hear their accusations about poor schedule development, but later found out why. I continue to be amused by those who think they have found a solution to networking through "backwards planning" or some 12 step process. Perfectly adequate processes for network development have been around for a couple of generations. If what I present here is not sufficient for your needs, read up on the practices, starting with the references I provide, and use them. The TOC Prerequisite Tree (PRT) can help to develop the WBS for some projects, but adds nothing beyond that to the state-of-the-art for building effective project networks.

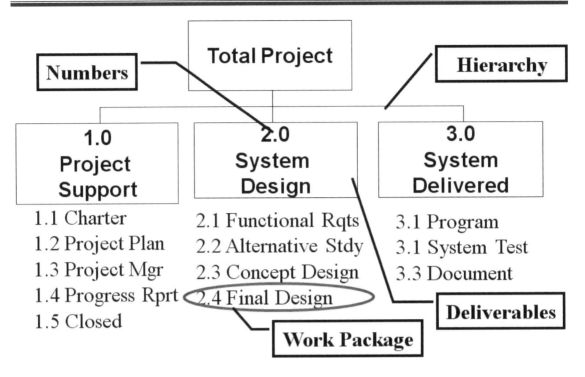

The Work Breakdown Structure (WBS) Drives Schedule Development. *The WBS defines the full project scope, assigns responsibility for deliverables, and integrates the schedule with other project elements, including budget.*

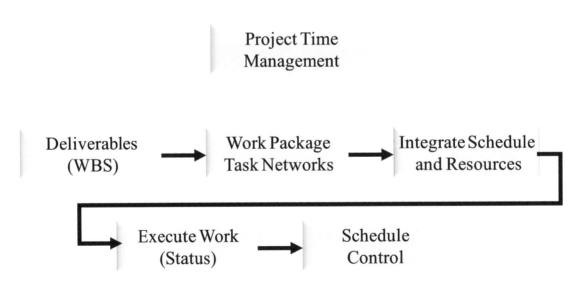

The Project Time Management Process. *Project time management starts with defining deliverables according to the work breakdown structure and ends with project control.*

Project Schedule

PMI states, "The purpose of scheduling is to provide a 'roadmap' that represents how and when the project will deliver the products defined in the project scope…" (PMI, p.1). While some call a project schedule a "plan", LPM considers it one highly important part of the Project Plan (see 5.6). The schedule:

1. Establishes the delivery date for the project and key milestones,
2. Dispatches work to resources,
3. Sets the baseline for project control,
4. Controls the flow of work in the project (synchronizes resources),
5. Provides a visual control means for the whole project.

The project schedule alone is insufficient for project control in most projects. For example, the Project Plan must specify the procedures for things such as quality assurance and the approval process for changes to the project, and an issue/action tracking tool must be used to aid resolving issues not specific to project tasks. Uttewaal provides an excellent source of information for project scheduling basics that are not unique to CCPM/LPM, including specifics that apply to scheduling with MS Project.

PMI. (2005). *Practice Standard for Scheduling*. Newtown Square, PA: Project Management Institute.
Uttewaal, E. (2005). Dynamic Scheduling. Boca Raton, FL: J. Ross Publishing

WBS

The Work Breakdown Structure (WBS) provides the backbone for integrating all elements of the project. It defines the scope of the project, responsibility for all project deliverables, and serves as the starting point to develop the project schedule. The WBS organizes the high level deliverables for the project in a hierarchy, and assigns responsibility for each deliverable to a work package manager. She develops the detailed schedule for that deliverable and manages the execution to create the deliverable. The WBS often links to a more detailed WBS dictionary or scope statement to clarify planning assumptions and deliverable details. The WBS normally should have less than ten level 2 elements. The PMI practice standard provides many useful examples and guidelines.

PMI. (2006). *Practice Standard for Work Breakdown Structures Second Edition*. Newtown Square, PA: Project Management Institute.

Assumptions

Project assumptions define an uncertain future as necessary to make a project schedule (and budget). Assumptions should reflect things you are at least 50% sure will be the case for your project. They may include constraints such as resources available. Identify assumptions at both the WBS level and the task level of the schedule. Consider key assumptions being wrong as project risks.

Work Packages

A work package creates one or more deliverables at the planning and control level of the WBS. A work package normally includes from one to twenty five tasks, and often includes milestones that can aid linking work packages together.

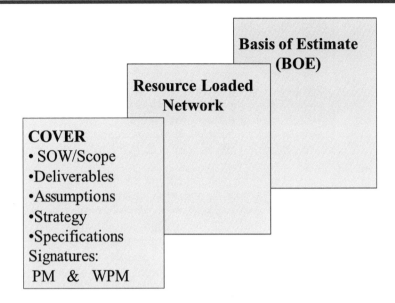

Work Packages Identify All of the Planning Information Required to Create the Project Deliverables.

Work packages roll up to summary tasks in larger project schedules.

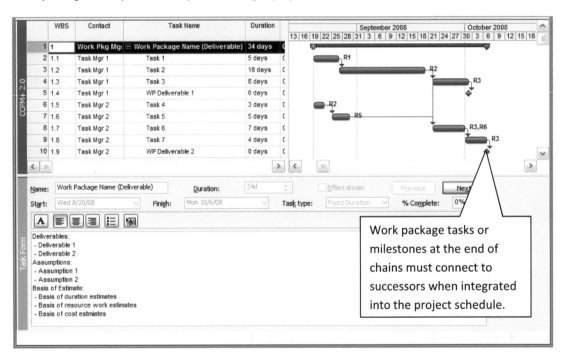

Work package tasks or milestones at the end of chains must connect to successors when integrated into the project schedule.

The Work Package Network Identifies the Task Workflow to Produce Work Package Deliverable(s).

Work packages may include technical milestones (without dates) and links to other work packages.

Work Packages

Work packages identify all of the tasks necessary to develop all of the project deliverables. Using the WBS and milestone sequence to link work packages comprises the overall project schedule network. LPM/CCPM networks seek to synchronize the flow of work. They avoid scheduling dates for each task. The workflow perspective usually demands fewer tasks in the network because the network primarily guides the hand-off of work from one resource to the next, like the passing of the baton in a relay race. It also simplifies the task relationships to only finish-to-start and eliminates the use of leads or lags between tasks. **DO NOT INPUT DATES ON NETWORK TASKS**…dates are outputs from the schedule calculation. The references below present some very useful network building information, but please use them with the perspective described above.

Larger projects usually provide a template for work packages identifying the work package manager, deliverables, requirements, assumptions, constraints, and often a formal basis for the task cost and schedule estimate. Smaller projects may include such information in the summary task notes field of the schedule or even forgo it.

PMI. (2005). *Practice Standard for Scheduling*. Newtown Square, PA: Project Management Institute.
Uttewaal, E. (2005). Dynamic Scheduling. Boca Raton, FL: J. Ross Publishing

Tasks

PMI defines activities (which I use interchangeably with tasks) as "element(s) of work performed during the course of a project. An activity normally has an expected duration, an expected cost, and expected resource requirements". Tasks usually require inputs from a predecessor task and create outputs that flow to a successor task or milestone deliverable. LPM associates a Task Manager with each task. Task Managers are accountable to plan and execute the task. They can be the same as the task Resource, but often are the supervisor of the Resource(s) that determine the task duration.

Relationships

Predecessor to successor relationships link tasks. The relationship means that the predecessor task creates an output that is a necessary input to the successor task. Most critical chain software limits you to finish-to-start relationships, with no lags. In reality, most project tasks can start with no or partial information from their predecessor task, and sometimes only need the final information to finish. When buffer management demands, you can take advantage of that flexibility.

Chains

The task relationships form chains of tasks. **All chains of tasks must lead to a single final milestone for the project**. All project tasks must lead to the final milestone so the software can calculate the critical chain. Each project schedule has one critical chain (see 3.2). All the other tasks are on feeding chains, connecting to the critical chain or the project ending milestone through a feeding buffer. Thus, all non-summary project tasks and milestones (except the final one) must have a successor. Tasks that start chains are the only ones that need not have a predecessor.

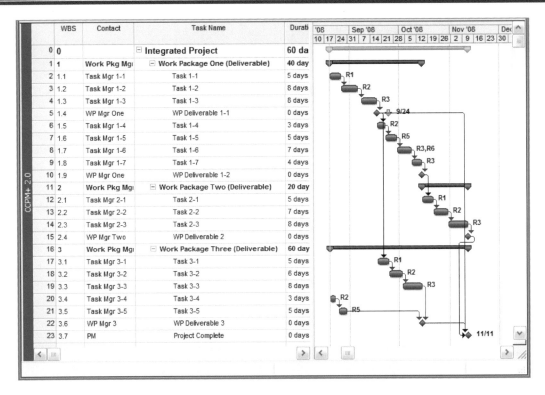

Integrated Schedule Network Sets Workflow for all Project Tasks. *Work packages roll up to summary tasks in larger project schedules.*

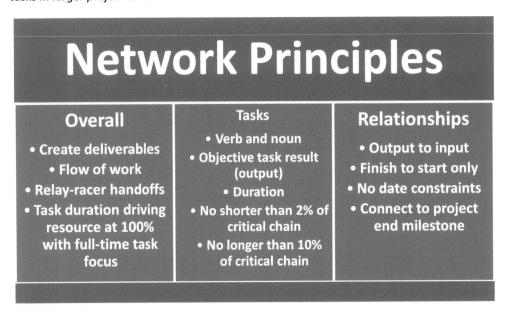

Principles to Ensure Effective Networks. *Focus on the flow of work.*

Integrated Schedule

The integrated schedule links all of the work packages to form a workflow for the entire project. Larger project schedules (i.e. more than about 50 tasks) should include milestones for key deliverables. Most of these milestones should not have dates.

Flow (Synchronization)

Integrate the network to ensure that the flow of work does not cause waste; in particular the waste of delay. The network must create 100% of the project deliverables, in the sequence that completes the project in the shortest time. It must minimize overloading resources, which causes queuing delay.

The tasks under each summary task should flow from the left to the right down the task list. This flow adds value along each chain of tasks connected by task relationships, where the output of a predecessor task(s) comprises the input to the successor task(s).

Detail

Project schedules must contain sufficient detail to guide the workflow. Keep in mind that if your project schedule is over 100 tasks, the average task represents less than one percent of your project…already too low a level of detail considering the variation in project tasks and the buffers that will be provided in the critical chain schedule. Very large and complex projects may require schedules at multiple levels, with the following guidelines applying to each level:

➢ Task duration should not exceed 10% of the critical chain duration.
➢ Task duration should not be less than 1-2% of the critical chain duration.

In order to achieve that, you can:

✓ Combine short tasks performed by the same resource in sequence.
✓ Divide tasks at intermediate deliverables.
✓ Include checklists within task notes or via. linked documents to provide additional detail where needed.

Guidelines

Consistent planning practices or guidelines simplify project execution. The figure lists the most important general planning practices. The most common problems are tasks:

✓ With date constraints
✓ Without successors
✓ Too-long duration (i.e. > 10% of critical chain)
✓ Short duration (i.e. less than 2% of critical chain)
✓ Series of tasks performed by the same resource
✓ Links to summary tasks
✓ Fractional resource loading for the resource that drives the task duration (fractional loading can be OK for support resources)
✓ Task network does not end in a single "project complete" milestone

Be sure to review your networks for these potential problems.

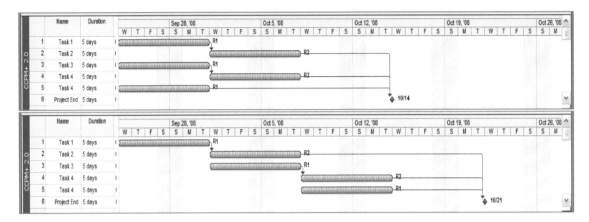

Resource Leveling Delays Tasks to Match Resource Demand to Resource Supply. *R1 and R2 are resources, each available at 100%. The upper illustration is before leveling, the lower illustration is leveled. Most software provides many options to drive leveling. Predicting the result of your choices can be difficult.*

Choose Simple Options for Resource Leveling. *If you have task durations less than one day, you must change the time basis to "hour by hour" or "minute by minute". This example is from Microsoft Project's leveling dialog. Be sure to click on **Level Now** to level: **OK** does nothing.*

Resources

Resources perform tasks by adding value to task inputs to create task outputs. Resources are usually the constraint to doing projects faster, and to performing more projects. Project schedules must be resource feasible to be achievable. Resources must have overall excess capacity to avoid long queues of tasks waiting to be worked. In LPM/CCPM, we assign a Task Manager as the one person accountable for a task. The Task Manager can be the resource that performs the task, but more often is the supervisor of that resource. Tasks can use multiple resource types and quantities.

Resource Loading

Resource loading identifies the resources necessary to perform project tasks. Most software allows hierarchical resource identification; e.g. you can identify "Senior Engineer", and under that have a list of the Senior Engineers. For larger organizations and projects, you should identify resources in the schedule by their generic title and enable the supervisor to assign tasks to individuals as the tasks come up to be worked. For smaller projects, or when only one resource has the qualifications, names are OK.

The resource that determines the task duration should be "loaded" to at least 100% (i.e. a full time person, fully focused on one task), or in multiples of 100%. Support resources can be at less than 100%, but you should generally not specify resources at less than 25%. The reason is that resource leveling will not overlay even a 1% loaded task with a 100% loaded task, which can lead to unnecessary planned project duration waste.

Resources are not limited to human resources. You can specify equipment or work areas as resources if they might be a constraint.

Resource Leveling

Resource leveling delays tasks to match the demand for resources to the availability specified in the resource pool. Project software usually provides several options for the resource leveling algorithm. Predicting the results can be difficult. Learn one that works for your projects, and stick with it. Only use more sophisticated options, e.g. task priority in MS Project, if absolutely necessary.

Guidelines

✓ Use standard project work time for all resources.
✓ The only non-working time should be shared by all; e.g. weekends and holidays.
✓ Load at least one resource per task at 100%.
✓ No resources less than 25% on a task.
✓ Do not "taper" resource loading.
✓ Do not use individual resource calendars.
✓ Account for non-productive time with the capacity constraint buffer.
✓ Only use priority or more complex resource leveling when absolutely necessary.
✓ When many people support a task; e.g. reviewing something, put them in task notes; not as resources.
✓ Expect some surprising results from resource leveling in the beginning. You will build the skill to avoid such surprises.

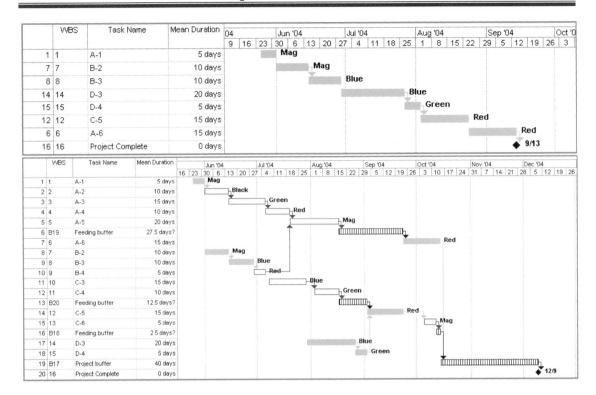

Initial Pass at a Critical Chain Schedule. *Note the tasks on the critical chain not connected by logic (e.g. WBS 1 and 2, WBS 8 and 14, and WBS 12 and 6), and the critical chain gaps introduced by buffer insertion.*

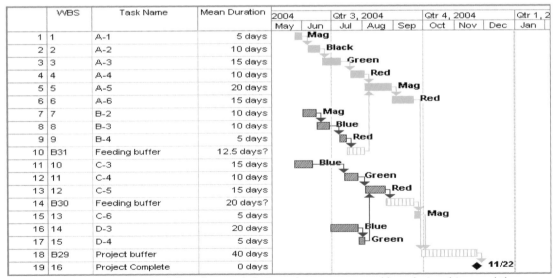

Optimized Critical Chain Schedule. *All critical chain tasks are connected by relationships, and there are no gaps in the critical chain. Note that the end date is 11/22, compared with 12/9 for the initial pass.*

Optimize

Optimizing a critical chain schedule means reducing the overall project duration to be as short as practicable without significantly increasing cost. Optimization starts with the critical path schedule, where the task durations have been adjusted, but resource leveling has not been applied. This is the shortest task schedule that your critical chain schedule can achieve. If it does not meet the target date, you need to start optimization with that critical path schedule. Optimization seeks to produce a schedule that is good enough to guide work flow. Good enough means you are unlikely to come up with additional changes that affect the schedule by about 20% of the project buffer duration. When you are initially satisfied with the critical path schedule, resource level the critical path schedule as per the previous section.

Critical Chain And Buffers

Next, develop the initial draft critical chain schedule by identifying the critical chain and inserting buffers. Identifying the critical chain should not affect the overall project's task duration. Inserting buffers extends the project duration by the addition of the project buffer, and often by inserting gaps into the critical chain. Inserting feeding buffers causes the gaps to appear in the critical chain.

Most critical chain software allows you to filter for the critical chain tasks only and sort the tasks by start date, showing the constraining flow of work for the project schedule. First check that the tasks on the critical chain are sensible; that they should be the set of tasks that determine the project duration. If not, go back to the critical path network and adjust relationships and resource loading until you get a reasonable set of tasks on the critical chain.

Resources

Then look for sequences of tasks on the critical chain that share a common resource, but do not have a predecessor-successor task relationship. These tasks present opportunities to shorten the project duration by changing the resources assigned to some of those tasks.

Guidelines

The following summarizes the optimization steps:
➢ Assure task predecessor-successor logic uses only necessary output-input task relationships.
➢ Eliminate tasks not necessary to the work flow; e.g. recurring tasks, Level of Effort (LOE) tasks.
➢ Ensure the schedule contains all tasks necessary to deliver the full scope.
➢ Use the critical path, before resource leveling, as the measure of "optimization" of the schedule.
   o If resource leveling extends end date by more than 20% of the project buffer, then look to change resources to reduce the critical chain.
   o Minimize gaps in the critical chain by revising relationships and resource assignments.
➢ If the final schedule does not meet the target end date, revise task linkages, resource assignments, and work processes until a satisfactory result obtains.

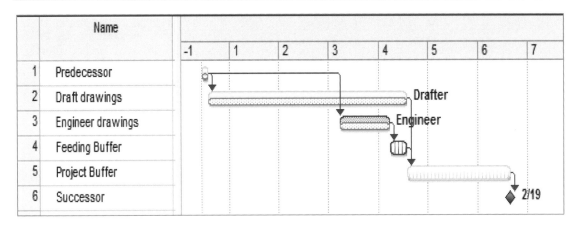

Parallel Tasks with Full Resource Loading and Common Predecessors and Successors. *The consequent placement of feeding buffers and status with remaining duration (The Engineer task will actually start before the drafter task) enables appropriate task priority and buffer impact. The Drafter task need not be on the critical chain as it is in this small example.*

Before SNET:

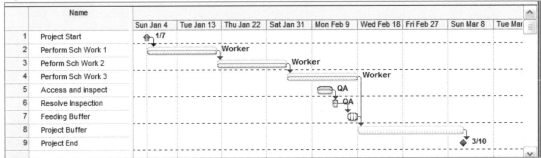

After SNET:

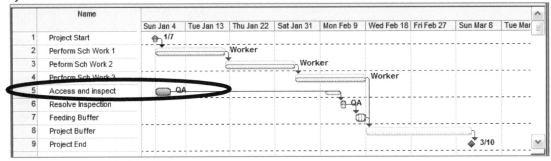

Risk Reduction Tasks Can Be Forced Early After Determining the Critical Chain Schedule. *Use the Start No Earlier Than (SNET) constraint.*

Optimize   Special tasks include all project work necessary to execute the project that does not fit into the flow of work, and special situation tasks that do fit into the flow of work.

Level of Effort   Level of Effort (LOE) tasks represent work that has to be accomplished over the life of the project, but are not part of the task output-input flow. LOE work includes:

> ➢ Administrative support to the project, including a project office.
> ➢ Technical support to the project that does not directly drive deliverables, such as quality, safety, or configuration management support.
> ➢ Ongoing project expenses, such as office rental or utilities.
> ➢ Project capital expenses, such as office equipment.

The project budget must account for the cost of these items, and project staffing must account for the resources needed, but the work tasks should not be part of the project schedule.

Recurring Tasks   Recurring tasks are things that happen on a periodic basis over the life of the project; usually weekly or monthly. Do not include these in the project schedule. They do not positively affect the work flow. You should include them in the standard procedures portion of the Project Plan.

Parallel Tasks   Tasks with widely different work loading by resources, but performed in parallel or on a basis of the resources passing back and forth to each other can be put in as one task with multiple resources, if the lower loaded resource is at least at 25%. If the loading for the lower loaded resource is much less, put in parallel tasks with common predecessors and successors, and load both at 100%. Statusing with remaining duration will create the proper task priority results.

Fixed Duration Tasks   Some tasks are actually fixed duration; e.g. a burn-in test or raising generations of laboratory animals. These tasks should be put into the schedule at their realistic durations, but not included in buffer calculations. The method for doing this depends on the critical chain software you use.

Risk Reduction Tasks   Risk reduction tasks must take place early in the project to allow for time to work adverse events. For example, maintenance and repair projects (e.g. ship or airplane overhauls) must open and inspect equipment and apply non-destructive tests to materials to determine if repair or replacement must take place during the overhaul. The project plan should assume the highest probability outcome for such inspections, which usually means no adverse findings. These tasks must take place at the beginning of the project to reduce the chance an adverse finding will affect schedule completion Thus, they are an exception to the "as late as allowed by resource leveling and Feeding Buffers" schedule default of LPM. Estimate the tasks with the most likely duration, include a very short duration task for the repair, should it occur, and then move the inspection task early in the project by applying a "start no earlier than" (SNET) constraint after establishing the critical chain schedule. If no repair is necessary, show the repair task as complete as soon as the result is found. Otherwise, use the remaining duration to track the actual repair task.

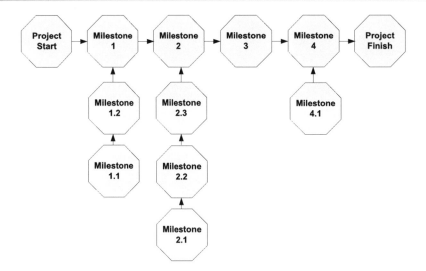

Milestone Sequence Establishes the Overall Workflow for Larger Projects. *Most milestones do not require fixed dates.*

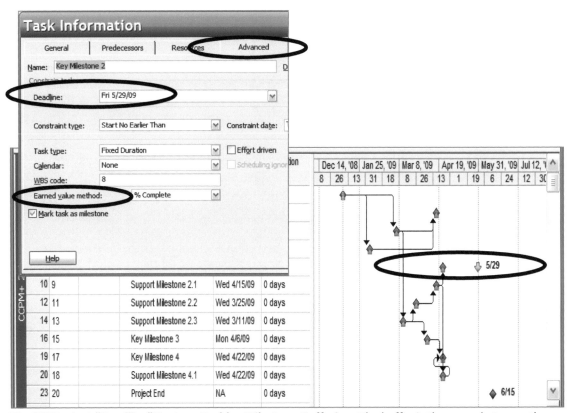

The MS Project "Deadline" Feature Enables Milestone Buffering. *The buffer is the space between the Milestone and the deadline symbol (down arrow). NOTE: All milestones need not be linked in the view shown, which is filtered to only show milestones.*

Milestones

Milestones are zero duration tasks. PMI defines them as "a significant point or event in a project". Milestones aid laying out the overall sequence of major work items in the project, starting with a "project start" milestone, and ending with the "project complete" milestone. Usually two hierarchical levels of milestones are sufficient, but very large projects may have more layers.

The PMI milestone definition, which works fine with LPM, *does not imply a deterministic date for a milestone*. Common practice usually assigns a deterministic date to milestones. There are situations where milestones require a fixed date, such as a date for a major meeting where venue arrangements are necessary and/or multiple parties must arrive at the same point at the same time, or where scheduling for another project must share a common resource, such as a dry-dock. The LPM rule is that any dates used as outputs from the schedule MUST have a buffer in front of them.

LPM has two types of milestones. The majority of LPM milestones will not have dates. The few that do have dates should use a milestone buffer to establish the deterministic date.

Milestone Sequence

For larger projects, a Milestone Sequence chart can aid schedule integration. The Milestone Sequence chart arranges the project's key events as predecessors and successors. Usually the key events are work package deliverables on the WBS. Create the Milestone Sequence after the WBS, but before adding tasks to the schedule.

Create the Milestone Sequence Chart with any drawing program, such as Visio. The chart is for the linkages; do not supply dates. If some milestones need dates, the dates should be outputs from the schedule, and include a buffer before the milestone.

Develop the Milestone Sequence with all of the project work package managers. Start with the key milestones across the top; the phasing of the high level flow of the project. Then determine the milestones necessary to support each of the key milestones.

Use the milestones on the Milestone Sequence chart when preparing the work package task networks. You can include milestones as inputs to start the flow of work in a work package, and as the culmination of the work in the work package. Then use the Milestone Sequence chart to aid linking work packages in the integrated schedule. All milestones other than the project end milestone must have successors in the schedule.

Milestone Buffer

Milestones that require fixed (deterministic) dates must have a buffer between the milestone predecessor and the date. One way to accomplish this in MS Project is to remove the dates from milestones by default, and use the "Deadline" feature, with a date, to display the buffered Milestone Date, as displayed in the lower figure. Other software may provide alternative means of illustrating the milestone buffer.

9. Improvement

It is, to some, a sad fact that the way of the world is such that all creations tend towards destruction. As an Engineer, I learned about this tendency as a law of nature in Thermodynamics. Entropy, the measure of disorder, constantly increases for all closed systems. It takes outside energy, or what is called an open system, to sustain the order of a system, and more external energy flow to improve it.

Once you have made improvements to your project delivery system with LPM, you have a choice. Because of the natural law described above, that choice does not include staying at the new improved level of performance. If you try staying where you are, your system will degrade. Your system MUST improve or die. Unfortunately, it also seems to be the natural tendency of people in organizations, once they have made a substantial improvement, to sit back and say "Whew". Then they see their system degrade over several years, before going back to improve it again.

When improving, the synergistic components of LPM provide a natural sequence to follow. I heard a speaker earlier this year pose a natural sequence for improvement and an acronym that contains the sequence: TLS, standing for TOC, Lean, and Six Sigma. The reason for the sequence is that TOC identifies the one place in the system that will create the largest improvement: the constraint. You can perform Lean and Six Sigma processes to improve non-constraints, but your organization will see little bottom-line impact from doing so. When you focus on the constraint, the organization immediately realizes more of the Goal.

The reason to move to the Lean ideas second, before Six Sigma, is that frequently the waste in the system dominates. You certainly do not want to improve processes in ways that maintain or increase the generation of waste. Then, once you have Lean processes, reducing variation in those processes moves the system further towards the Lean goal of perfection.

I offer one caveat to the above. The Lean and Six Sigma approaches to improvement tend towards incremental improvement. Incremental improvement is not, by itself, a bad thing. I recall a case made by Dr. W. Edwards Deming to show that incremental improvement, compounded over time, can have much more effect than large improvements spaced over time…to say nothing of the cost of failed attempts at large improvements. Edward deBono illustrates with many examples how such incremental improvement most often leads to diminishing returns, and always will lead to the end of a particular trail, after which only a new foundation, an entirely new direction to achieve the goal, can lead to substantial further improvements. I recommend Edward DeBono's works as a starting point.

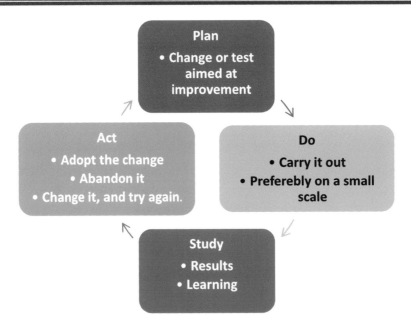

The Plan, Do, Study, Act Process Drives Continuous Improvement. *Deming called it the Shewhart cycle. Japan calls it the Deming cycle. Deming originally called it the PDCA (Check) cycle. The Six Sigma DMAIC process elaborates on it.*

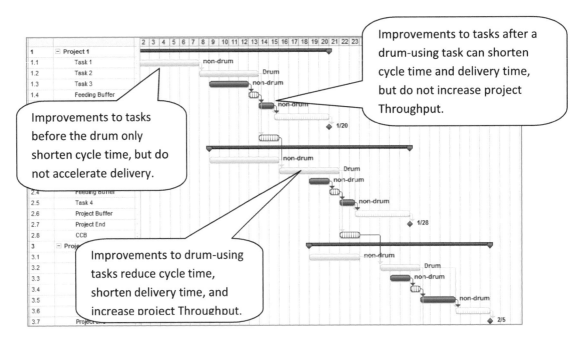

TOC Guides the Direction of Improvement, focusing the Six Sigma and Lean Tools. Only Improvements to the Drum-resource-using tasks map directly to Throughput Improvement.

Ongoing

Ohno notes, "Progress cannot be generated when we are satisfied with existing situations" (p. 107). Dissatisfaction is the first step of ongoing improvement. Sustaining a culture of ongoing improvement challenges many organizations. Many organizations make a substantial leap in performance with LPM/CCPM, and then stagnate at that new performance level. Ongoing improvement must be a continuous process to prevent degradation.

Ohno, T. (1988). Toyota Production System. Portland, OR: Productivity Press

What to change?

TOC leads the way to determining where to focus ongoing improvement efforts. Most local sub-system improvements have little impact on the goal or critical success factors for the organization. *Strategic Navigation* provides one of the more powerful TOC approaches to decide where to focus. *Strategic Navigation* starts with periodic resetting of the organization's goal and identifying the critical success factors (CSFs) and conditions necessary to achieve the new performance level.

The metrics installed as part of an effective LPM/CCPM can help focus on the changes that will most impact the organization's goal. For example, improvements in processes performed by the drum resource translate immediately into Throughput improvements, while changes that affect non-drum tasks may only improve the cycle time of individual projects. Improvements to tasks upstream of the drum-resource-using tasks have no effect on due date performance.

Use the overall schedule and cost control charts for project buffer consumption at completion to decide when your process is afflicted with special causes and also to drive reduction of overall project delivery variation.

Pareto charts can aid identifying the types of tasks or resources that most often impact the project buffer, further focusing your improvement efforts. Control charts on individual tasks can help focus local improvements to reduce variation, but be cautious as most such improvements will add little to the bottom line.

Dettmer, W. (2003). Strategic Navigation. Milwaukee, WN: ASQ Press

What to change to?

Once the system is operating to the LPM/CCPM paradigm, what directions of change are likely to be productive? Some that I consider likely are:

1. Focusing on goals other than profit; e.g. environment impacts and harmony among people.
2. Enhancements to customer satisfaction with project results.
3. Simplified processes.
4. Joyful communication.
5. Improving the project scheduling process.
6. Enhancements to workflow to reduce defects and delays.
7. Further reductions of variation in task and project performance.
8. Further reductions of waste in task and project performance.

I believe that there are improvements to be made that will far exceed the improvements achieved with LPM/CCPM.

How to cause the change?

The processes described in section 7 of this workbook apply to any type of improvement.

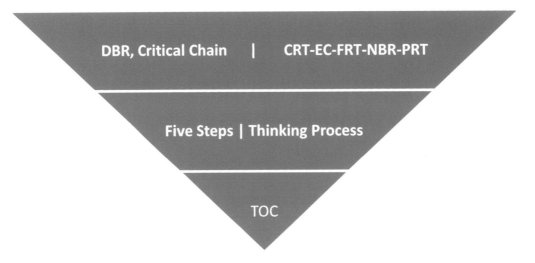

TOC Provides a Series of Tools for Ongoing Improvement. The most important tool is the simple realization of the constraint to flow of a system, followed by the five focusing steps to deploy that understanding.

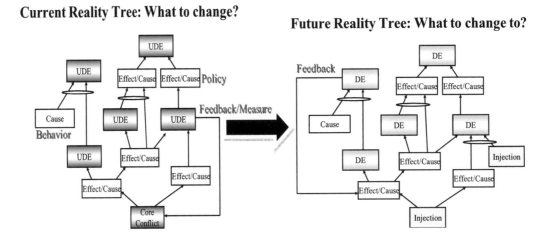

The TOC Thinking Process Focuses System Improvements through a Core Problem or Conflict (aka root cause). The process proceeds from identifying the Undesired Effects (UDEs) afflicting current reality to a coherent strategy and synchronized plan to cause the desired changes.

TOC

The Theory of Constraints (TOC) provides a number of specific improved processes, such as critical chain, and several powerful system improvement tools. The Five Focusing Steps provide the first and simplest system tool. Simply asking, "Where is the constraint to the flow of this system" can often lead to focusing positive changes at the only place they matter. The rest of the tools are logical diagrams depicting effect->cause->effect, and methods to develop and deploy them. They function as stand-alone tools for specific purposes or link together as the TOC Logical Thinking Process (LTP). While the LTP is logically attractive, few demonstrate the necessary knowledge, skill, and stamina to apply it all the way through to breakthrough levels of system performance. The tools aid thinking through any problem.

Individual LTP tool elements have much greater use and success as stand-alone tools. The Evaporating Cloud (EC), a conflict resolution tool, and the Prerequisite Tree (PRT), a team focusing tool, are the ones I use the most. Goldratt first described these tools in his novel *It's Not Luck*.

What to change?

The LTP begins by developing a map of current reality: the Current Reality Tree (CRT). CRT development first defines the system goal and the Undesired Effects (UDEs) that currently afflict the system. Applying the TOC assertion of inherent simplicity means that all of the UDEs of the system are linked and that in most cases one can find a root cause which TOC calls a core problem or core conflict that can lead to changing all of them. This identifies where to start to the change and an analysis of the conflict at this point leads to an initial Injection (change in the system) to begin to bring about an improved system.

Several approaches have been used to identify the core conflict. The initial approach built downwards from the UDEs to find a core problem and identify the conflict that allows that core conflict to exist. The second approach first developed three conflicts directly from the UDEs and sought to construct an underlying core conflict from them. Current approaches develop systemic and symptomatic conflicts directly from the UDEs.

Dettmer, W. (2008). The Logical Thinking Process. Milwaukee, WN: ASQ Press

What to change to?

The Future Reality Tree (FRT) identifies the desired future system, in which Desired Effects (DEs) replace all of the UDEs of the current system, starting with a few Injections. It starts with the injection for the core problem or conflict and adds others as necessary to convert all UDEs of the CRT to DEs in the FRT. FRT development identifies feedback loops and necessary new policies, behaviors and measures. Final development of the FRT includes Injections to prevent unintended consequences using a process of identifying potential Negative Branch Reservations (NBRs) with the initially proposed changes; i.e. instances where changes introduced for a positive effect can lead to an unintended negative consequence.

How to cause the change?

The Prerequisite Tree (PRT) links and elaborates on the Injections of the FRT with Intermediate Objectives (IOs). The linked IOs comprise a coherent strategy for a synchronized plan to bring about the future reality. The final planning step converts the PRT to a CC schedule and project plan to cause the change, using the LPM project delivery process and the organization change process of section 7.

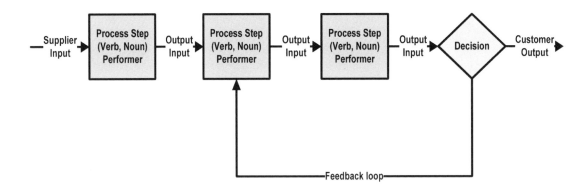

Process Management Begins With a Process Flow Chart or Process Map. The process map links process steps. Process steps include Supplier, Input, Process, Output, and Customer for the process result. Links between steps identify the supplier (predecessor step) and customer for the process (successor step). Process flow charts show decisions and feedback looks.

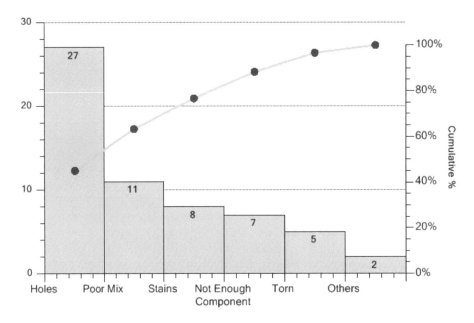

The Pareto Chart Aids Identifying Main Causes of Buffer Penetration. The ordinate sums days of buffer penetration, the abscissa categories can be type of task, performing resource, or reason for buffer penetration (e.g. lack inputs, multitasking demands, missing resource, etc.). The Pareto guides applying root cause analysis tools, including the cause-and-effect diagram or the TOC TP tools, to identify what to change to improve the process.

Six Sigma

Ohno notes, "In business, excess information must be suppressed" (p.30). Six Sigma applies a range of tools, from simple charts to sophisticated statistical methods. It is easy to get lost in the detail of analysis. Be sure to first focus on the constraint and how to improve its Throughput.

Details of the sophisticated statistical tools are beyond the scope of this text. My purpose is to focus on the tools necessary to improve the project delivery system. Improvements to the project delivery system focus on the Throughput of the system, where Throughput implicitly includes quality products that satisfy customer needs.

Ohno, T. (1988). Toyota Production System. Portland, OR: Productivity Press

Basic Tools

Two of the most basic improvement tools emphasized by W. Edwards Deming are process flow charts and run charts. Process flow charts are essential to understanding a process for improvement, and to help identify the constraint. Process flow charts apply at both the overall project delivery system level, and at the levels of the individual project tasks and operational control mechanisms; e.g. the change management process. Run charts are the first basic step to collecting time series data for subsequent analysis and control. The most basic run charts for LPM are project schedule performance (schedule buffer penetration at project completion), cost performance (cost buffer penetration at project completion), and an appropriate quality measure, e.g. number of defects. Run charts are easily converted to more useful control charts as processes are brought into statistical control.

Seven basic tools of quality assurance have been used in wide application, to include:
1. Cause-and-effect diagram (aka Fishbone or Ishikawa diagram): determines the likely cause of out-of-control process conditions.
2. Pareto chart: categorical histogram, to identify the most significant contributors to an effect. Use in LPM to identify the primary contributors to buffer penetration.
3. Check sheet: used to assure quality; e.g. list of the inputs necessary for a project task.
4. Histogram: charts the distribution of data from a process, e.g. the actual duration of project tasks, or the ratio of actual to planned duration.
5. Scatter diagram: x-y plot to determine the relationship between two variables; e.g. actual task duration vs. estimates task duration.
6. Control chart (3.4.2): used to control both the project delivery process and the processes that comprise tasks. The most basic ones in LPM are the ones for schedule and cost buffer penetration at project completion.
7. Various graphs.

Advanced Tools

Advanced Six Sigma tools apply various tools, from Kano requirements definition (Pande et. al. 89-91) and Failure Modes and Effects Analysis (which applies to project risk management), to sophisticated statistical tools, including Design of Experiments (DOE) for optimizing processes or products.

Pande, P., Neuman, R. and Cavanagh, R. (2002). The Six Sigma Way Team Fieldbook. New York: McGraw-Hill

10. Future Direction

You have reached the end of what I presently have to offer on LPM and its component parts. There is a lot there, and I am sure I could work the rest of my life perfecting many elements of the material covered in this book. But that is not enough for me, and I know it is not enough for many of you.

First, I do not think improving work on projects is enough. I know it is not enough for the organizations that perform both project and non-project work. While I know that focus works equally well for all work, a process is needed to get the non-project work prioritized for execution relative to the project work. I am not satisfied with our processes for doing that yet.

Second, I have throughout this work assumed that the projects that are on the plate are the right projects. I know that is sometimes not the case. Even when the problems or opportunities that the projects are planned to address are the right ones, or at least good ones, I know that that the chosen solutions are often far from what could be achieved with more focused up-front thinking, applying tools like TRIZ or those offered by Edward deBono.

Finally, because I think it most important, I don't feel as though any of the improvement approaches do enough for people. Although all improvement approaches espouse considerations of psychology, and some of sociology, somehow ologies seem to me to lose the people. Where is what the Dali Lama calls Loving-Kindness, or Compassion? Where is saving the earth for future generations? Where is saving mankind from itself? Where is relieving suffering?

I think all of us can be leaders when it comes to what matters most. That is the direction I am heading, and I invite you all to come along. Or, I will be happy to go along with you if that is the direction you are going. Please contact me with your thoughts on this, and together we can work to make a better world for everyone else, now and in the future.

Larry Leach

September 20, 2009

Email me at: Lawrence_leach@hotmail.com

The best leaders are those the people hardly know exist.
The next best is a leader who is loved and praised.
Next comes the one who is feared.
The worst one is the leader that is despised.
If you don't trust the people,
They will become untrustworthy.
The best leaders value their words, and use them sparingly.
When she has accomplished her task,
the people say, "Amazing: we did it, all by ourselves!"

Tao Te Ching on Leadership.

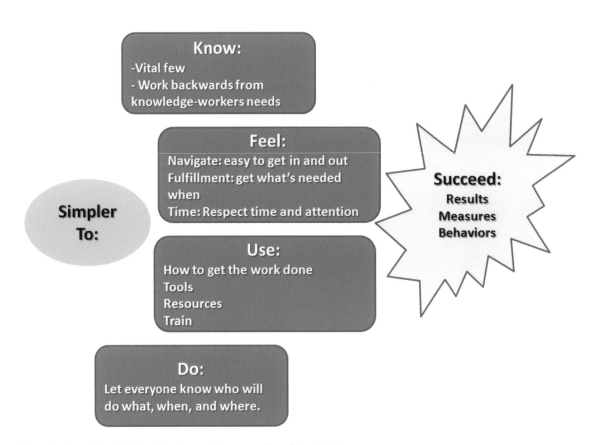

Designing the Project Delivery Process for Simplicity.

The Chinese symbol represents harmony, the theme of the magnificent 2008 Beijing Olympics. My vision of future project delivery systems includes elegance, harmony, beauty, and related things, creating universal happiness for all touched by the system. I feel this means moving towards simplicity and ever improving leadership. Simplicity means simple to learn, apply, and achieve outstanding results for all.

New "Agile" methods of software development demonstrate a movement in that direction. The Agile approach turns the conventional approach to planning and executing software upside down; replacing complicated "waterfall" schedules for large scale IT implementations with a *people-centered process* to develop useable software modules. Similar approaches are needed in other types of projects.

Tao Te Ching defines my vision of the direction for project leadership (see figure across). Written by Lao-Tzu in the 6th century B.C., it applies as well now, but unfortunately still more often as a vision than as reality.

Simplicity
Wikipedia defines simplicity as "*the property, condition, or quality of being simple or un-combined. It often denotes beauty, purity or clarity. Simple things are usually easier to explain and understand than complicated ones. Simplicity can mean freedom from hardship, effort or confusion.*"

Simplicity is often contrasted with simplistic. Einstein noted, "*Things should be made as simple as possible, but not simpler*". John Seely Brown, a chief scientist at Xerox's think tank PARC noted, "*Keeping things simple is profoundly misunderstood. If you begin by honoring the social mind, you engage in what I call cognitive judo. You let the world do more of the work for you. Follow that principle and things that were hopelessly complicated actually start to straighten out in a very interesting way*" (Jensen, p. 12). Dr. Eliyahu Goldratt defines inherent simplicity in terms of Newton's claim that "*Nature is exceedingly simple and harmonious with itself.*" He notes that, when looking at apparently complex systems more closely, "[we believe] *we will end up with more and more causes to deal with; the intuitive impression is that systematically using "why?" will just lead to more and more complexity. What Newton tells us the opposite happens; the system converges; common causes appear as we drive down*". This perspective can lead to elegant solutions.

Jensen, B. (2000) Simplicity. Cambridge, MA: Pegasus Publishing
Goldratt, E. (2008). The Choice. Great Barrington, MA: North River Press

Elegance
Breakthrough solutions require looking at a problem domain a new way. Future improvements must reflect the ever changing complexity of reality, where everything connects. Often one cannot progress in small steps from an excellent old way to a vastly improved new way…quantum leaps require new perspectives. We cannot extrapolate from the past into that new future.

Paradoxically, creating simplicity may not seem simple. DeBono notes, "*There is often a much simpler way of doing things—if you make the effort to look for it. Simplicity does not just happen*". (p. 2). Finding simple, elegant, harmonious solutions requires perceiving the problem or system from another perspective; usually from that of the user. DeBono provides many tools to help you lead in that direction; in particular with his lateral thinking and six thinking hats.

DeBono, E. (1998). Simplicity. London: Penguin Books

LPL Acronym List

ABC	Activity, Behavior, Consequence model of behavior reinforcement
AC	Actual Cost: PMIs new term for ACWP
ACWP	Actual Cost of Work Performed
BAC	Budget at Completion
BCWP	Budgeted Cost of Work Performed (EV)
BCWS	Budgeted Cost of Work Scheduled
CC	Critical Chain
CCB	Capacity Constraint Buffer
CCFB	Critical Chain Feeding Buffer
CCPM	Critical Chain Project Management
CCRB	Critical Chain Resource Buffer
CCRT	Communication Current Reality Tree
CLR	Categories of Legitimate Reservation
CPI	Cost Performance Index
CPM	Critical Path Method
CRD	Conflict Resolution Diagram: See EC
CRT	Current Reality Tree
CSCS	Cost Schedule Control System
CV	Cost Variance
DBR	Drum-Buffer-Rope
DE	Desired Effect
DMAIC	Six Sigma Improvement Process: Define, Measure, Analyze, Improve, Control
DOE	Department of Energy
EAC	Estimate at Completion
EC	Evaporating Cloud
EV	Earned Value (BCWP) (Also see BCWS, ACWP, CV, SV, SPI, CPI)
FB	Feeding Buffer

FRT	Future Reality Tree
I	Inventory: in TOC, all of the money invested to produce Throughput. I includes WIP.
IO	Intermediate Objective
LCL	Lower Control Limit
LOE	Level of Effort
LPL	Lean Project Leadership (or Lawrence P. Leach)
NIC	Negative, Immediate, Certain consequence to a behavior.
NP	Net Profit
OE	Operating Expense
OPM3	Organizational Portfolio, Program, and Project Management
PB	Project Buffer
PERT	Program Evaluation and Review Technique
PDSA	Plan, Do, Study, Act
PIC	Positive, Immediate, Certain consequence to a behavior.
PMBOK	Project Management Body Of Knowledge
PMI	Project Management Institute
PMP	Project Management Professional
PRT	Prerequisite Tree
PV	Planned Value: the PMIs new acronym for BCWS
QFD	Quality Function Deployment
RACI	Responsibility, Accountability, Commuicated, Informed
RCA	Root Cause Analysis
RDU	Remaining DUration
ROI	Return on Investment
SIPOC	Supplier, Input, Process, Output, Customer
SNET	Start No Earlier Than
SOW	Statement (or Scope) of Work
SPI	Schedule Performance Index
S&T	Strategy and Tactics
SV	Schedule Variance

T	Throughput
T/C	Throughput per unit of Constraint Use, usually $/hour
TIP	Tasks in Progress
TM	Task Manager
TOC	Theory of Constraints
TP	Thinking Process
TQM	Total Quality Management
TRT	Transition Tree
UCL	Upper Control Limit
UDE	UnDesired Effect
WBS	Work Breakdown Structure
WIP	Work in progress. For projects, all of the work that has been performed on projects not yet complete.
WP	Work Package
WPM	Work Package Manager

LPL Glossary of Terms and Dictionary

ABC Model
Model of behavior in which antecedents precede and consequences follow and reinforce behavior.

Activity
The lowest level of the work breakdown structure (WBS); a packet of work that forms the basic building block of a plan or network. An activity usually requires inputs, is a process step, always creates an output, and usually has resources and duration assigned to it. I usually define activities with at least a two-word pair: verb-noun, with the verb describing the process within the activity. Interchangeable with task.

Activity network
A network made up of two or more activities with a precedence relationship.

Additional Cause Reservation
One of the Categories of Legitimate Reservations used to scrutinize logic trees. The reservation means that the causes posed are insufficient to cause the predicted effect.

Antecedent
Circumstances, including signals and signs in our internal and external environment, which set the occasion for behavior.

Balanced scorecard
This is a strategic management system used to drive performance and accountability. It balances traditional performance measures with more forward-looking indicators, such as finances, integration and operational excellence, employees, and customers.

Behavior
Any activity of a living creature.

Behavior Analysis
A field of study that uses the principles and techniques of science to determine the relationships between behavior and its interaction with the environment.

Behavior Chain
A sequence of behaviors in which the reinforcer for one behavior serves as an antecedent for a subsequent behavior.

Benchmarking
This is an improvement process that an organization uses to compare its performance against best-in-class companies. It then uses the information gathered to improve its own performance. Subjects that can be benchmarked include strategies, products, programs, services, operations, processes, and procedures.

Black Belt
Six Sigma team leaders responsible for implementing process improvement projects to increase customer satisfaction levels and business productivity are known as "Black Belts." They are knowledgeable and skilled in the use of Six Sigma methodology and tools, typically have completed 4 weeks of training, and have demonstrated a mastery of the subject matter through the completion of projects and an examination.

Bottleneck
The constraint to Throughput in a production flow process. The limiting capacity process step.

LPL Glossary of Terms and Dictionary

Buffer

In process inventory, time or budget allowance used to protect scheduled throughput, delivery dates, or cost estimates on a production process or project.

Buffer Management

- Weekly updating and communication of project's buffer status by asking "how many working days to complete?" for all tasks currently in work, and projecting buffer penetration.
- Actions by Project Managers in response to the buffer report. If buffers are green, Project Managers should take no action. If yellow, they should plan how to recover time by looking down the chain from the current working task. If red, they should implement the recovery plan.
- Actions by task resources to select which task to work on next when presented with multiple tasks. Resources should work on critical chain tasks over non-critical chain tasks. If presented with multiple critical chain tasks, or multiple noncritical chain tasks, resources should work on the task with the greatest % buffer penetration.

Buffer Penetration

The amount of buffer projected to be consumed comparing the current status of the project network, actual durations for completed activities, projected days to complete for working activities, and estimated (mean) duration for future activities. Sometimes called Buffer Incursion.

Capacity

The ability of a resource to produce. For personnel resources, the capacity is usually expressed as a "headcount" or "full-time-equivalents" (FTEs).

Capacity Buffer

aka Capacity Constraint Buffer (**CCB**) The buffer that sequences projects. It is part of the Drum schedule. Size the capacity buffer to at least 25% of the drum resource capacity.

Categories of Legitimate Reservation (CLR)

A simplified set of logical fallacies used to check the logic of TOC causality trees. The CLRs commonly include:
- Clarity
- Entity Existence
- Causality Existence
- Insufficient Cause
- Predicted Effect
- Additional Cause
- House-on-fire

Causality Reservation

Concern that the posed causality does not exist in reality.

Cause

An entity that inevitably leads to a certain result (effect). Causality is determined if the predicted effect is always present when the cause is present and never present when the cause is not. Causes may be single or may require other conditions to lead to the effect.

LPL Glossary of Terms and Dictionary

Cell

A cell is a group of people, machines, materials, and methods arranged so that processing steps are located adjacent to each other and in sequential order. This allows parts to be processed one at a time or, in some cases, in a constant small batch that is maintained through the process sequence. The purpose of a cell is to achieve and maintain an efficient, continuous flow of work.

Clarity Reservation

Concern that an entity is a logic tree is not clear. Common clarity reservations include use of acronyms, too brief a description of the entity, and including 'and' in the entity.

Cloud (EVAPORATING)

See Evaporating Cloud.

Communication Current Reality Tree (CCRT)

A CRT with an Evaporating Cloud at the base, originally developed to present current reality to a specific group of people for buy-in. The CCRT presents the Evaporating Cloud in sufficiency form, adding entities as necessary to do so. For most TOC applications, the CCRT has replaced the CRT in the Thinking Process. Development of the CCRT starts with identifying three Evaporating Clouds to address three UDEs, and then generalizing those clouds into a Core Conflict.

Conflict Resolution Diagram (CRD)

Another name for the Evaporating Cloud.

Consequence

Something that happens as a result of an action or behavior.

Constraint

In general systems thinking, a limit to a system entity or relationship. In TOC, the process or process step that limits Throughput. In CCPM, the Critical Chain of a single project, or the Drum Resource in a multi-project environment. In project terminology, limitations placed on scheduling a task; e.g. 'Start no earlier than.

Continuous flow

Each process, whether in an office or plant setting, makes or completes only the one piece that the next process needs; the batch size is one. Single-piece flow, or one-piece flow, is the opposite of a batch-and-queue process.

Core Conflict

The conflict placed at the bottom of a CCRT, from which many or most (at least 2/3) of the UDEs stem.

Core Problem

A primary cause of most of the UDE symptoms in your system. You identify the Core Problem as an entry point on your CRT that traces, in cause-effect-cause relationships, through at least 2/3 of the UDEs, and which you have the stamina and energy to change.

LPL Glossary of Terms and Dictionary

Cost Buffer

The contingency or management reserve added to the sum of the project's mean task cost estimates to create the project baseline budget. You can use the cost buffer to manage project cost. Cost buffer penetration is the cost variance from earned value: See the Project Management Institute's Project Management Body of Knowledge (PMBOK) or other project resources to understand Earned Value.

Critical Chain

The longest set of dependent activities, with explicit consideration of resource availability, to achieve a project goal. The Critical Chain is NOT the same as you get from performing resource leveling on a critical path schedule. The Critical Chain defines an alternate path which completes the project earlier by resolving resource contention up front.

Critical Chain Feeding Buffer (CCFB)

A time buffer at the end of a project activity chain which feeds the critical chain.

Critical Chain Project Management (CCPM)

A complete system of effective project management integrating the Critical Chain method of project time management with the other elements of the Project Management Institute's Project Management Body of Knowledge (PMBOK™), and considering the elements of Total Quality Management (TQM).

Critical Chain Resource Buffer (CCRB)

Originally an indicator associated with tasks on the critical chain to notify resources that a critical chain task is coming up for them to work on. This buffer is insurance of resource availability, and does not add time to the critical chain. It takes the form of a contract with the resources that ensures their availability, whether or not you are ready to use them then, through the latest time you might need the resource. Often shortened to Resource Buffer, and sometimes called Resource Flag. Rarely used in this form: the prioritized task list by resource has replaced that functionality. Some are now introducing a different resource buffer concept: having a "SWAT" team of highly skilled resources, not assigned to project tasks, available to assist buffer recovery.

Critical Path

The longest set of dependent activities in a project, not accounting for the resource constraint. See the Project Management Institute's Project Management Body of Knowledge (PMBOK) or other project resources to understand critical path

Current Reality Tree (CRT)

A sufficiency tree connecting together all of your UDEs on a particular system. The CRT is the first step in the Thinking Process, and is created to identify the Core Problem of your system, and to aid in developing your Future Reality Tree.

Cycle time

This is the time a person needs to complete an assigned task or activity before starting again.

LPL Glossary of Terms and Dictionary

DBR
Drum-Buffer-Rope method for production scheduling. The drum is the capacity of the plant constraint, and is used to set the overall throughput schedule. The buffers are in-process inventories strategically located to eliminate starving the constraint due to statistical fluctuations. The rope is the information connection between the constraint and material release into the process.

Dependent events
Events in which the output of one event influences the input to another event.

Desired Effect (DE)
The positive effect you want to have in Future Reality to replace your UnDesired Effect of current reality.

DMAIC
This acronym stands for "define, measure, analyze, improve, and control". It is the heart of the Six Sigma process and refers to a data-driven quality strategy for improving processes. It is an integral part of any company's Six Sigma quality initiatives.

Drum
The bottleneck processing rate, which is used to schedule an entire plant. Also refers to the bottleneck work station. In CCPM, the resource used to stagger the start of projects. It should be the most highly used resource, and one that is not easy to elevate.

Drum Buffer
Buffer placed in the project plan immediately in front of the first use of the drum resource in a project. Its purpose is to enable project acceleration if the drum resource is available early. Size the Drum Buffer as a feeding buffer for the preceding chain in the project. Drum buffers only exist in a multiple project environment. Drum buffers are the least important buffer, and are used infrequently.

Drum Manager
In Critical Chain, the manager responsible for allocation of the drum resource. The Drum Manager creates the Drum Schedule, which is used to sequence the start of projects.

Effect
An entity representing the result of one or more causes.

Elevate
The TOC term for increasing a resource.

Entity
A condition that exists.

Entry Point
An entity on a sufficiency tree which has no causes (arrows) leading into it.

LPL Glossary of Terms and Dictionary

Evaporating Cloud

A process for conflict resolution consisting of a five entity necessity tree and processes for developing and communicating to achieve win-win solutions to any conflict.

The action alternatives are best expressed as opposites e.g., 'Do D, don't do D." The cloud has five entities and arrows: A, the *goal*, B and C, the two *needs* that must be met by D and D', respectively. Goldratt called D and D' prerequisites; but *wants* or *initial alternatives* works better for me. You identify the assumptions underlying the arrows to resolve the cloud. You develop injections that will invalidate the assumption, and therefore invalidate the arrow and 'dissolve' the cloud.

Existence Reservation (Entity or Causality)

This means, "Prove it." Following Popper's elaboration of the scientific method, such proof is the result of critical discussion and/or experiment. While you can never prove reality, you can prove that this statement of reality is operationally more effective than alternative theories.

Exploit

In TOC, getting the most out of the constraint resource, in a positive sense, directed at the goal.

Feeding Buffer

See Critical Chain Feeding Buffer.

Five (5) S's

Five terms beginning with "S" are used to create a workplace suited for visual control and Lean production.

- **Sort** (Seiri). Eliminate everything that is not required for the current process and keep only the bare essentials.
- **Straighten** (Seiton). Arrange all items so that they are easily visible and accessible.
- **Shine** (Seiso). Clean everything, and find ways to keep everything clean. Make cleaning a part of everyday work habits.
- **Standardize** (Seiketsu). Create rules by which the first three S's are maintained.
- **Sustain** (Shitsuke). Keep 5S activities from unraveling. (i.e. form the inner habit of performing the first four)

Five (5) Whys

The "5 Whys" typically refers to the practice of asking 5 times why a failure has occurred in order to get to the root cause of any problem. Of course, a problem can have more than one cause. Generally, root cause analysis is carried out by a team of people who are related to the problem. No special technique is required.

Five Focusing Steps

- **IDENTIFY** the constraint to the goal
- **EXPLOIT**
- **SUBORDINATE**
- **ELEVATE**
- Do not let **INERTIA** prevent you from doing it again.

LPL Glossary of Terms and Dictionary

Float
In critical path, the difference in path length between the critical path and converging path. Also called slack. Float is often confused with Feeding Buffers. It is not the same. Float is an accident of the network logic, and has nothing to do with the uncertainty of the duration of the tasks in the chain. Float varies inversely with the necessary size of feeding buffers, and thus does not provide protection for uncertainty in task duration.

Flush
A project measure for making decisions. Flush is the time integral of net profit times days, in units of dollar-days.

Future Reality Tree (FRT)
The system model of the desired final state of a system, showing the Desired Effects (DEs), and the logic, including Injections, necessary to create and maintain the future system state.

Goal
The purpose for the existence of a system; or the single end that the system seeks to maximize. For profit making companies, the goal is to make money now and in the future. Not-for profit companies have alternative goals, usually expressible in terms of Throughput related to their purpose. Most organizations have a set of necessary conditions required to achieve the goal, usually including necessary conditions 1 and 2 (See in glossary).

Goal, The
Book by Dr. Eliyahu M. Goldratt.

Green Belt
A Green Belt is an employee who has been trained on the Six Sigma improvement methodology and will lead a team. The degree of knowledge and skills associated with Six Sigma is less than that of a Black Belt or Master Black Belt. Extensive product knowledge is a must in a green Belt's task of process improvement.

Heijunka
This Japanese term refers to the act of leveling the variety or volume of items produced by a specific process over a period of time. This system is used to avoid excessive batching of product types or volume fluctuations, especially with a pacemaker process.

Hockey Stick
The shape of a curve that is relatively flat and then rises rapidly, representing, for example, the amount of effort one puts out as a deadline approaches.

House-on-Fire-Reservation
A logical error: affirming the consequent. "If there is smoke, then the house is on fire."

Injections
Changes in reality that will lead to desired effects. Injections may be actions or Intermediate Objective.

Intermediate Objective (IO)
An action or effect which is a necessary prerequisite to an injection or another IO.

LPL Glossary of Terms and Dictionary

Inventory All of the money a system invests in things it intends to sell. In TOC, it extends beyond the conventional definition to include all the items traditionally considered as depreciable assets. For projects, there may be value in considering the work invested in projects as Inventory until the project is complete, and it begins to produce Throughput.

JIT "JIT" stands for "just in time." This means producing or conveying only the items that are needed by the next process when they are needed and in the quantity needed. This process can even be used between facilities or companies.

Jonah Character in The Goal. Title awarded to those who complete the AGI 'Thinking Process' training.

Kanban This is a signaling device that gives instructions for production or conveyance of items in a pull system.

Kaizen "Kaizen" is the Japanese word for improvement. However, it implies more than improvement in the basic production processes. Kaizen represents a philosophy by which an organization and the individuals within it undertake continual improvements in all aspects of organizational life, based on the idea that a process is never perfect.

Lean A manufacturing philosophy to produce more with less, commonly linked to the Toyota Production System (TPS). The primary thrust of Lean manufacturing is to eliminate waste.

This is simply a thought process, not a tool. The key thought processes within Lean are identifying waste from the customer's perspective and then determining how to eliminate it.

Lean Project Management (LPM) The synthesis of Lean manufacturing ideas with CCPM, considering the enhanced principles of Six Sigma quality management.

Master Black Belt These are Six Sigma quality experts who are responsible for strategic implementations within an organization. Their main responsibilities include training and mentoring of Black Belts and Green Belts; helping to prioritize, select, and charter high-impact projects; maintaining the integrity of Six Sigma measurements, improvements, and "tollgates" (control points); and developing, maintaining, and revising Six Sigma training materials.

Material flow The movement of a physical product through the value stream.

Mean The average of a group of data, also called the first moment of the data population. In a distribution skewed to the right, as most duration and cost estimates are, the mean is higher than the median. Mathematically, mean durations should be used on the Critical Chain, as they are the only statistic that adds linearly.

LPL Glossary of Terms and Dictionary

Median
The middle value of a group of ordered data. The median is the '50/50' probability statistic, often confused with the mean or the mode.

Mode
The most frequent value of a population.

Muda
The Japanese word for waste. Lean identifies seven types of Muda:
- **Overproduction** ahead of demand.
- **Waiting** for the next processing step.
- Unnecessary **transport** of material
- **Overprocessing** of parts.
- **Inventories** above minimum.
- Unnecessary **movement** by employees.
- **Defective** parts.

Necessary Condition #1
Satisfy customers now and in the future. (A necessary condition to meet the Goal of any enterprise.)

Necessary Condition #2
Satisfy and motivate employees now and in the future. (A necessary condition to meet the Goal of any enterprise.)

Necessity Tree
A logic tree in which each item at the tail of an arrow MUST exist in order for the item at the head of the arrow to exist, BECAUSE of some assumption or obstacle represented by the arrow.

Need
A requirement which MUST be met in order to achieve an objective or goal.

Negative Branch
A sufficiency logic tree (potential FRT) stemming from an INJECTION which leads to unintended negative consequences.

Negative Reinforcement
Strengthening of behavior when that behavior results in the escape or avoidance of something aversive.

Obstacle
An entity, which prevents an effect from existing.

One-piece flow
In its purest form, one-piece flow means that items are processed and moved directly to the next station one piece at a time. Each processing step completes its specific work just before the next process needs the item; the transfer batch is one.

Operating Expense
All of the money it costs to convert raw material into throughput.

Opportunity cost
This is the foregone value of an alternative that is precluded by choosing another alternative. Other types of costs may include variable, fixed, direct, indirect, period, and product.

Overproduction
This is the process of producing more, sooner, or faster than is required by the next process or customer.

LPL Glossary of Terms and Dictionary

Parkinson's Law
"Work expands so as to fill the time available for its completion." Parkinson, C. (1957). *Parkinson's Law*. Cutchogue, NY; Buccaneer Books.

Pipelining
The implementation of pull in a multi-project system by sequencing the start of projects to the capacity of the constraint resource (drum).

PMBOK™
Project Management Body of Knowledge: The Project Management Institute's description of a complete project management system. (See www.PMI.org)

Positive Reinforcement
The process of strengthening behavior by following it with a positive reinforcer.

Predicted Effect Reservation
One of the CLRs challenging entity existence and/or causality existence on the basis of the lack of an inevitable effect that would have to exist if the entity existed. This is perhaps the most powerful CLR, representing application of the scientific method. The draft tree is the hypothesis, and you are seeking to invalidate it by critical discussion and perhaps even test.

Prerequisite Tree (PRT)
A logic tree representing the time phasing of actions to achieve a goal, connecting intermediate objectives with effects that overcome obstacles. The PRT is read, "In order to have ENTITY AT HEAD OF ARROW we must have ENTITY AT TAIL OF ARROW because of OBSTACLE."

Priority
The priority assigned to a project, used to determine access to the drum resource. Priority should be based on the expected project Throughput per unit of drum resource consumption. The Drum Manager uses the project priority and project schedules to level demand on the drum resource by sequencing the start of projects.

Procedure (Poka Yoke)
This is a mistake-proof device or procedure designed to prevent a defect from occurring throughout the system or process.

Productivity
This is the ratio of measured outputs over measured inputs, such as the number of widgets produced per man-hour.

Project Buffer (PB)
A time buffer placed at the end of the critical chain in a project schedule to protect the overall schedule.

Project Charter
The first document prepared for a project. It guides the team to plan the project. It includes the mission or purpose for the project (Why), the general scope, identifies the project team and stakeholders, and provides other key project parameters necessary to plan the project, such as key assumptions.

Project Execution Plan
aka Project Plan, Project Management Plan, Project Work Plan: The plan for the project, describing scope, budget, schedule, the project team, project stakeholders, and project control.

LPL Glossary of Terms and Dictionary

Pull	One of the Lean principles, describing the manufacturing process of downstream processes informing upstream processes when to produce another part. In CCPM and LPM, Pipelining of projects implements Pull.
Quality Function Deployment (QFD)	Akao, Y. (1990). Quality Function Deployment. Norwalk: Productivity Press, defines it two ways: 1. QFD (narrowly defined): The business or task function responsible for quality (design, manufacturing, production, etc.), 2. QFD (*broadly* defined): A combination of the business or task functions responsible for quality (design, manufacturing, production, etc.) and the quality deployment charts.
Queuing	The lining up of work to be processed by a server (resource).
Red curve-Green curve	The Red Curve represents the typical process of ongoing improvement, which increases for a while and then decreases.
Reinforcement	The strengthening of behavior by following it with positive or negative reinforcers (consequences).
Relay Racer Behavior	The task behavior expected of each individual working on Critical Chain projects, in which they: • Start a task as soon as they are available and have all of the inputs, • Work on only that one task applying 100% of their work effort, and • Pass on the result of their work as soon as they complete it. If presented with multiple tasks to work on, resources exhibiting Relay Runner Behavior use the Buffer report and buffer management rules to decide which task to work on next.
Resource Allocation	Assigning resources to project tasks.
Resource Buffer	A buffer associated with critical chain tasks to reduce queuing delay for work on critical chain tasks. Originally conceived as a warning device to alert resources to upcoming critical chain tasks. Supplanted in most instances by filtered prioritized lists of tasks for all resources.
Resource Leveling	Adjusting a project plan such that the plan demanded resources do not exceed the available resources.
Roadrunner Behavior	See Relay Racer Behavior. Roadrunner was the initial metaphor suggested, but some feel that the cartoon it is based on is not the best description of the performance expectation.
Root Cause	The cause which, if changed, will prevent recurrence of an UDE. The same as the TOC Core Problem.
Root Cause Analysis (RCA)	Assessment of system performance to aid prevention of negative consequences.
Rope	The information flow from the Drum (bottleneck resource) to the front of the line (material release) which controls plant Throughput.

LPL Glossary of Terms and Dictionary

Scrutiny — Inspection of a tree to ensure that none of the categories of legitimate reservation apply, and that all of the entities are necessary to connect the UDEs.

Sequencing — Scheduling the start of projects to not overload the drum resource.

SIPOC — Acronym for a way of presenting a process and/or process steps:
- Supplier
- Input
- Process
- Output
- Customer

Six Sigma — A process improvement process focused on reducing variation. Six Sigma refers to having less than 3.5 defects per million opportunities, considering that the mean of a statistical distribution can vary by plus or minus one sigma. The Six Sigma process is designed to eliminate variances in a process in order to allow the best flow of work using the necessary analytical tools and processes.

Standard work — This term refers to a precise description of each work activity's cycle time, "takt time" (see below), sequence of specific tasks, and the minimum inventory of parts needed on hand to conduct the activity.

Statistical fluctuations — Common cause variations in output quantity or quality.

Student Syndrome — The natural tendency of many people to wait until a due date is near before applying full energy to complete the activity.

Subordinate — In TOC, enabling exploiting the constraint to the goal by not allowing other things to prevent its exploitation. For example, not allowing efficiency measures to cause ineffective operation of a system to achieve the goal.

Sufficiency Tree — A tree construction in which the existence of the entities at the tail of the arrow make the existence of the entity at the head of the arrow an unavoidable result.

Supermarket — This is a very visible, controlled inventory of items that is used to schedule production at an upstream process.

Systemic Conflict — A conflict inherent in an organization system leading to many of the Undesirable Effects of a system. Systemic conflicts differentiate from symptomatic conflicts because the systemic conflicts are usually not immediate to any one symptom (UDE). Sometimes also called "latent causes", because they are usually not immediately visible. Systemic conflicts usually associate with the core problem of a system.

LPL Glossary of Terms and Dictionary

Takt time   This is the rate of demand from a customer. Takt time equals the available operating time or requirement.

Task   See activity.

Theory of Constraints (TOC)   A system theory developed by Dr. Eliyahu Goldratt, and first published in his book <u>The Goal</u>, based on the principle that complex systems exhibit inherent simplicity. The most basic statement of the theory is that

a) systems are defined by a single goal, and

b) the output of a system is limited by a constraint.

Even very complex systems can have, at any point in time, only a very small number of variables, often only one, that limit the ability to generate more of the system's goal.

Thinking Process   The five step process which identifies What to change?, What to change to?, and How to cause the change? There are two prerequisites to apply the Thinking Process. You must first:

- Define the system (which requires defining its Goal and boundaries).
- Create operational measures for the Goal.

The Thinking Process uses the following tools:

- Evaporating Cloud
- Current Reality Tree (CRT)
- Future Reality Tree (FRT)
- Negative Branch (NBR)
- Prerequisite Tree (PRT)
- Transition Tree (TRT)
- Categories of Legitimate Reservation (CLR)
- Communication Trees (TRTs to apply the Thinking Process, CCRTs, and CFRTs)

The initial Thinking Process applied the Evaporating Cloud after using the CRT to determine a Core Problem. The current method starts with three Evaporating Clouds to pose a Core Conflict, and builds the initial CRT as a CCRT. Dettmer adds the word Logical to Thinking Process.

Throughput   The rate at which the system makes money or other goal unit of measure. All of the money (or other goal measure) our customers pay us (demand) minus the raw material cost.

Transition Tree (TRT)   An effect plan specifying the effects to be achieved, the starting conditions, the actions necessary to create the effects, the logic of why the action will create the effect, and the logic for the sequence of the effects.

LPL Glossary of Terms and Dictionary

Upper Control Limit (UCL)	The upper line on a control chart, used to signal a data point that is likely from a special cause of variation. Also called the upper Natural Process Limit (NPL).
Undesired Effect (UDE)	UDEs are negative effects of the system that exist in reality, and about which you can say, "It really bothers me that UDE." UDEs must be negative in and of themselves; i.e. they should prevent you from achieving more of the Goal of your system, including blocking one or more of the necessary conditions for the Goal. Note that UDEs are EFFECTS. They cannot contain 'IF..THEN' statements.
Value	This term refers to a product or service capability that is provided to a customer at the right time and at an appropriate price.
Value stream	This term encompasses all activities, both value added and non-value added, that are required to bring a product, group, or service from the point of order to the hands of a customer and a design from concept to launch to production to delivery.
Value stream mapping	This is a pencil-and-paper tool used to— • Follow a product or information (or both) activity path from beginning to end and draw a visual representation of every process—whether value added and non-value added—in the material and information flows. • Design a future-state map that has waste removed and creates more flow. • Produce a detailed implementation plan for the future state of the organization.
Visual Control	A Lean philosophy to simplify control for the workers with effective visual displays.
Want	The effect that one believes MUST exist in order to satisfy a need, because of some set of ASSUMPTIONS.
Waste (Muda)	Waste includes anything that does not add value to a final product or service, such as an activity that the customer would not want to pay for if it knew it was happening.
Waste types	Sources of waste can include overproduction, excess inventory, defects, overprocessing, unneeded motion, wasted employee talents, waiting, transport delays, and reprioritization actions.
WIP (Work in Progress)	These are items—material or information—that are between machines, processes, or activities waiting to be processed.

LPL Glossary of Terms and Dictionary

Work Breakdown Structure (WBS) A hierarchical representation of the deliverables of a project. The starting point for project scope definition and integration of the project.

Work Package A grouping of one to around twenty-five project tasks to enable effective network planning and control during execution. A work package may have some similarity to cell in production.

Sources include:

1. API TOC Dictionary from www.advanced-projects.com

2. TOC International Certification Organization draft dictionary from http://tocico.org

3. The **ARMY LOGISTICIAN,** PROFESSIONAL BULLETIN OF UNITED STATES ARMY LOGISTICS, Published NOVEMBER–DECEMBER 2006

4. Daniels, A. and Daniels, J. (2006). Performance Management Changing Behavior That Drives Organizational Effectiveness. Atlanta, GA: Performance Management Publications

5. Various other publications

LaVergne, TN USA
16 February 2011
216813LV00005B